# LEECHES AND BREECHES

# F. V. SQUIRES

Edited by
J. R. L. Anderson

Published & Distributed in Great Britain in 2015
by
RED CAP PUBLISHING
100 Marlborough Gardens, Faringdon, Oxfordshire, SN7 7DN
+44 (0) 7435456010
Email: info@redcappublishing.com
Copyright © Dick Squires 2014, 2015

The right of Dick Squires to be identified as the author of this work has been asserted by him in accordance with the Copyright, Designs and Patents Act 1988.

The copyright holder assumes all liability for this book and indemnifies the publisher against all claims arising from its publication. All aspects of the work, including permission to use previously published material, are solely the responsibility of the copyright holder.

A CIP catalogue record for this book is available
from the British Library.

ISBN   978-0-9931642-2-4

All rights reserved. No part of this publication may be reproduced, stored in a retrieval system or transmitted in any form or by any means (electronic, mechanical, photocopying, recording or otherwise) without the prior written permission of the copyright holder.

Edited by J.R.L. Anderson
Design by Stuart Roper


Cover & all images by Dick Squires

# Contents

Chapter 1   Early Days in Cambridge
Chapter 2   World War I
Chapter 3   Embarkation for the Western Front and Wounded
Chapter 4   Invalided Back Home
Chapter 5   St Thomas's Hospital
Chapter 6   Visiting Australia
Chapter 7   Start of General Practice in Wantage
Chapter 8   Responsibilities
Chapter 9   Private Life
Chapter 10  War Again
Chapter 11  Hospital Ship
Chapter 12  Italy and Yugoslavia
Chapter 13  Home Again
Chapter 14  After the War and the National Health Service
Chapter 15  Fall and a Broken Neck
Chapter 16  Summing Up

# Preface

In the late sixties I was talking to my old patient J. R. L. Anderson about the extraordinary life of my father who had lived through so many changes in the course of his lifetime. He suggested that he could help me write his memoirs as he had experience as a correspondent with the *Manchester Guardian*.

My father was born at the end of the nineteenth century in Cambridge, where he enjoyed a gentle middle-class upbringing with a slightly hopeless solicitor father whose partner embezzled a large portion of the firm's money. His mother was a more charismatic figure, whose family came from Australia. She insisted that all the debtors were fully reimbursed. So life was necessarily simple with economies to be made and transport mainly still by horse and cart.

At seventeen he was called up as soon as he reached university in Cambridge and was almost immediately engulfed in the horrors of war.

He survived but only just, lying wounded all day in the main square of Arras with his leg and side of his body full of shrapnel. He eventually recovered and resumed his studies a year later, qualifying as a doctor.

Further adventures in Australia followed until eventually he returned to England, joined a practice in Wantage, marrying the local games mistress and settling down to family life.

All too soon the Second World War was looming and he volunteered, feeling perhaps in need of a bit of excitement in his life. He was soon working as a surgeon on a hospital ship, ferrying the wounded from Italy to North Africa. He kept a faithful diary, hiding it each night in a box of X-ray plates as a diary was strictly forbidden. Somehow he survived all sorts of really hairy situations and emerged after the war to re-join the practice, taking part in the beginning of the NHS.

He settled back into the everyday life of the sleepy little town, his excitement being riding his beloved horse to the hunt. This was nearly his undoing as he broke his neck when he was in his sixties, but he survived once again to carry on (just about) in general practice.

By this time (the 1960s) I had joined the practice and realized how little I knew of his early life and decided to interview him every day after lunch. I spent the evenings getting some sort of order and writing up what he had told me. I have included the large wodge of wartime diaries in his memoirs.

Initially it was very difficult and disruptive as he needed a pee every few minutes but I found it much easier when I fixed him up with an indwelling catheter which drained into a bag strapped to his thigh.

His memories of the First World War were crystal clear but most of the years in general practice had merged into a bit of a blur, although he was amazed that men had landed on the moon.

After the end of each week I handed my writings to John Anderson who corrected my appalling grammar and spelling to match. The script in longhand was then passed to John's wife, Helen, who kindly typed it for me.

*Dick Squires*

# Chapter 1

# Early Days in Cambridge

It used to be open house on a Sunday afternoon at Chesterton Manor, Cambridge where the Bells lived. Charles Todd who was an astronomer at the Greenwich Observatory had come down from London to visit his aunt and was telling her about his exciting new appointment to the Cambridge Observatory as assistant to the Rev. Prof Challis.

"With a job such as that you will have to get married," said his aunt.

"Good heavens, get married. No one would want to marry a boring chap like me."

"I would, Mr. Todd," replied a voice from under the tea table. Alice Bell, aged 12, was discovered hiding, and was reprimanded by her mother for being so impertinent.

"I would love to marry you my dear," replied Charles Todd, "But we will have to wait till you are a little older."

Six years later, when he was at the Cambridge Observatory, Charles Todd did marry Alice Bell, neither of them having the least idea that her name would find its way on to the map of Australia as the "Alice" of Alice Springs.

In 1854 Charles Todd was offered the post of Government Astronomer and Inspector of Telegraphs of Southern Australia. This he accepted and in the following year (1855) they left London Docks in the sailing barque *Irene*. The voyage to Australia took six months, and when they landed they settled into the Observatory near Adelaide. Their first daughter, Charlotte Elizabeth, the eldest of six children, was born two years later. She was destined to be my mother.

Charles Todd did not return to England for twelve years, when, accompanied by his eldest daughter, he attended an international conference to discuss the possibilities of linking the whole continent of Australia with London by cable. The telegraph cable then reached only as far as Java. A submarine link to Darwin in Northern Australia was within the bounds of what was then technically feasible, but it was considered an enormous task to continue the cable overland 2,000 miles across the unsurveyed middle of Australia to Adelaide in the South. My mother's

*Charles and Alice Todd*

BACK L-R - Mrs Charles Edward Todd (nee Elise Beatrice Backhouse), W. H. Bragg (Prof at Adelaide Uni, later Sir Wm and Nobel prize winner jointly with his son, for Physics, 1915), Alice Maude Mary Todd (later in 1900, married Rev. F. G. Masters), Mrs Mabel Tower (nee Backhouse and sister to Elise), Hedley Laurence Todd (married 1892), Lorna Gillam Todd.
MIDDLE L-R - Lady Alice Todd (nee Gillam Bell, married 1855), Gwendoline Bragg (nee Todd, married 1889), Dr Charles Edward Todd (married Elise), Charlotte Elizabeth Squires (nee Todd, married Charles Squires 1885), Mrs Hedley Todd (nee Jessie Scott), Sir Charles Todd, KCMG, FRS, FRAS.
FRONT L-R - William Laurence Bragg (later Sir Laurence, joint winner with his father of Nobel Prize for Physics, 1915), Frances Tower, Yolande Tower, Robert Bragg (killed WW1).
TODD CHILDREN - Charlotte Elizabeth, Charles Edward, Hedley Laurence, Alice Maud Mary.

3

most abiding recollection of that first trip to England was of the chickens (kept for fresh meat) on board the boat. They were penned in coops underneath the deck-seats, and used to peck her bare legs as she sat there.

Charles Todd arrived back in Australia in 1868, full of enthusiasm for the cable project, but he was met with considerable scepticism by people who doubted if such a feat of overland cable-laying was possible. Eventually it was decided that the route would be divided into three sections, Northern, Central and Southern. He was to appoint someone to be in charge of each section, and the whole link was to be completed by 1872. The Southern and Central sections were finished on time but the contractor for the Northern section went bankrupt because of the appalling conditions of drought interspersed with floods, bad food, heat and sick animals. Charles Todd then took over direction of the work himself, and carried it through successfully. He wrote many letters back to "My Dearest Alice" at the Observatory in Adelaide from his camp on Roper River and the party leader, William Mills, named a pool of water in the centre of the Australian bush "Alice Springs".

A few years later Charlotte Elizabeth Todd sailed again for England

*H.C. Squires, my father*

to stay with a wealthy friend of her father, a Mr. Openheimer of Stockport. All I can remember my mother saying about Mr. Openheimer was his strange habits with the ladies. He was a bachelor, but had a housekeeper. For his summer holiday he would go on a continental tour taking with him three attractive young women and enjoy walking round ballrooms with a different girl on his arm each evening.

My mother also visited her relations, the Bells, at Chesterton Manor and it was here, at one of the Sunday afternoon tea parties, that she met my father, a young solicitor. He had been brought up with his brother Stewart on their uncle's farm, because his father had died leaving his mother penniless, and the kindly uncle said he would take the two boys into the farm and feed them in return for work on the land. My father always longed to go to Cambridge, and with great determination he saved up his pocket money for books to teach himself Latin and Greek. Eventually he attained the standard required to pass the "Little-Go" examination, and entered Downing College. On coming down from Cambridge he was articled to a Cambridge solicitor and on qualifying he went into partnership at 11 Bennett Street. He lived with his mother at Langfield Road but he would often walk over to the Bells at Chesterton Manor for Sunday tea.

My mother shared with her father a natural ease when talking to people, being interested in what they had to say and making them feel that really they were not as stupid as they thought. At one time my grandfather had been invited to dine with Queen Victoria at Buckingham Palace.

"What on earth did you talk about?" my mother asked.

"Oh I just told her a few of the funny things that you do and she roared with laughter," he replied.

I can imagine the impression that my mother must have made on that first encounter with my father – he a shy, awkward young man, who had had little time for anything except working on the

*Alice, Stenie and myself*

farm and reading books, and she a much travelled young woman from far off Australia with two voyages to England, and wide experiences. After about two years my father summoned up enough courage to ask Elizabeth Todd to be his wife, and they were married in 1877, in Stockport at Mr. Openheimer's house.

Throughout the whole of their life my parents lived at Vale House, Cherry Hinton, Cambridge, a three storied heavy Victorian building. Although my father earned only about £500 a year, he could afford a cook, housemaid, gardener, and, later on, a nanny, paying them about 10/- a week. My father was in partnership with a rather flashy man, totally unsuited to his own very cautious temperament, who lived in great style in a large house in Cambridge.

About five years after their marriage, disaster fell on the family - the flashy partner disappeared one morning taking with him a large proportion of the clients' money, and leaving my father to cope with the situation. My father reacted to this by going to bed with a phenacetin cachet and a vinegar rag on his forehead, leaving my mother to face swarms of angry clients who came to the house. She told them patiently and bravely that if only they would wait, all money owing would be paid in full. There followed years of struggle, as my mother and. father met the demands of an increasing family, and pinched and scraped to pay back every penny of the debts left by my father's defaulting partner.

I was born on June 15 1895, my parents' third and last child. When my mother's labour pains started my father set out to walk 2½ miles to fetch the doctor (Dr Deighton). But the doctor was out, so my father sat on the doorstep to wait for his return. Meanwhile at Vale House, old Mrs. Baldock, the verger's wife, had arrived to pay a social call; finding my mother about to give birth she rolled up her sleeves and delivered me. By the time Dr Deighton and my father got there, I was born.

I was christened Frederick Vaughan. Why Frederick, I don't know, but the Vaughan was after one Vaughan Harley (of Harley Street) who was a friend of my mother's and whom she asked to be my godfather. He responded by saying that he did not want to see me, let alone to be my godfather - but I was stuck with his awful name.

My mother, having been used to taking the lead in society in Australia, took the lead with great determination at home when there was no money. One looks back on that vanished world before the First World War with a sense of unreality, but we had a succession of maids from a certain Mrs. Pluck, who herself approached my mother asking if her daughters could go into service with her, observing "I like my daughters to go into service with people from titled folk because they are the folks who know how to behave." My grandfather having been knighted by Queen Victoria we were, I suppose, connected with "titled folk". Anyway, the girls were well trained and well looked after - and whatever the supposed horrors of domestic service I remember our maids as happy, smiling girls.

We children were looked after for most of our time by our plump round-faced nanny, Carie Grass, who was very kind and affectionate. We adored her. Nanny had an admirer, James Hicks, who lived in the Fens and used to call in for tea at Vale House when he came in for market. We enjoyed his visits, because then we would have sausages for tea. The village where he lived was called Felt Well - and it was not until years later that we realised the significance of this name.

Dr Deighton was keen to have children's tonsils removed. My elder brother was seven when he was taken along to the surgery to have his tonsils taken out by the guillotine apparatus, with no anaesthetic; and then he had to walk the 2½ miles home. I was terrified that I would have to undergo a similar operation, but luckily I kept my tonsils and adenoids. I did, however, have a hernia repaired at home with an anaesthetic of open ether administered by Dr Deighton's partner, Dr Wingate. I was looked after by a wonderfully kind young nurse who lived in our house for three weeks. While she was staying with us she received the horrifying news that her father, a Protestant landowner in Ireland, had been assassinated. A political group had apparently broken into his house early one morning, woke him up, taken him into his garden and ordered him to dig his grave before shooting him and burying him.

The first school I went to was run by Miss Hutt at Linwood House, but known locally as Putty Guts. The school was about 2½ miles away and I had to walk there each morning and back in the evening. I objected so strongly to the grey rice pudding which we were given that my mother allowed me to come home to lunch - which meant another 5 miles walking every day, 10 miles in all. Bullying was rife and on the way to school a gang of older boys used to lie in wait for me, sometimes knocking me to the ground with kicks and punches. Then I would have the added anxiety of arriving at school filthy and bruised, to meet the wrath of Miss Hutt. One morning my elder brother, Stenie, came with me, and when we drew level with the usual ambush and the boys leapt out at me Stenie rushed at them and knocked them down one by one. This was the last time they lay in wait for me.

I was not quick at learning, but I used to plod on at a subject and eventually get the answers. It was always my ambition to be top of the class, and I had a great surge of joy when I saw myself first at the end - of - term marks at Putty Guts. I rushed home from school to tell my mother that I was first, and would be getting the form prize. Here, at last, I felt, was some compensation for all the bullying I had had. To my dismay, however, when the prize-giving came, the form master announced that "Squires, although he was first, had not worked hard enough and the prize would be given to the pupil who was second." When I got home mother asked me where the prize was, and I had to make feeble excuses, saying that they had kept them until next term to engrave our names on them.

It was with great relief that I left Putty Guts to go to St Faith's. The fees were 11 guineas a term which my father said he could not afford but my mother was determined. The academic standard was high and higher in some subjects than I ever reached at public school. One piece of extravagance my father indulged in was my knickerbockers suit. My father was keen that I should be dressed as he felt a proper young gentleman should be, so he had a knickerbockers suit made for me at his tailor's, Mr. Waites, off St Andrew's Street. It was the best Harris Tweed, a heather mixture, impregnated with the aroma of the moors. On my arrival at school, feeling rather self conscious, the other boys were not as impressed as my father, and formed a crocodile behind me shouting "Stinky Squires, stinky Squires."

My father had indeed a rather awkward approach to people, even his own family. He knew that I had long wanted a bicycle with pneumatic tyres, but when he eventually bought one for my tenth birthday he could not give it to me directly, but left it in the field behind our house, leaning against a fence, and then said to me, "Look around old fellow, look around! Perhaps you will find something you might like." That bicycle was marvellous for me, and I spent many happy days in the holidays on it.

The whole family was keen on sketching and I often used to get up early and set off on my bicycle with my watercolours and a stool. I used to wear a black cape, tying the apron of the cape to the handlebars of the bicycle, making a hammock for our little terrier Nick. I used to cycle for miles like this to sketch churches and landscapes, especially in the St Ives, Huntingdon direction. I would draw the subject one day and come back the next to complete the watercolour. Once when I had cycled nearly 20 miles each way with Nick in the cape I let him loose as we approached Cambridge to have a run alongside the bicycle. A bystander shouted at me saying how cruel it was to make a poor little dog run like that! I was much upset by this. We had to walk or cycle everywhere in those days, for there were no buses until 1906, when a company began running a motor bus – a very modern invention - from Cambridge to Cherry Hinton. The bus would leave the middle of Cambridge at 1 p.m. to travel the three miles to Cherry Hinton: but often it would be late in the evening before it returned, accompanied by mechanics, and with the passengers pushing. In our younger days we counted it a great treat to have a ride in a cart belonging to Nellie Moden, the washerwoman. She would come to our house to collect the washing once a week, and return it two days later. Even my mother, who was on calling terms with the wife of the great Master of Trinity, J. J. Thomson, was not above getting a lift from Nellie Moden. All dressed up in her best coat and skirt, and wearing a big hat, she would sit beside Nellie to be taken on her way to pay a call.

Everyone in those days had an "At Home" day. My Mother's was Friday and on Fridays our drawing room was always full of people who were already friends, or who wanted to meet mother. With her romantic Australian background, and her easy manner with people, she was a popular figure in our society. My mother's sister in Australia, Gwendoline Todd, had married a brilliant young scientist who held the post of Professor of Physics at Adelaide University. He was William Bragg, later to become Sir William, and world-famous. In 1909 the Braggs decided to come back to England with their three children, William Laurence, Bob, and Gwendy. They travelled in the *Waratah*, a smart new ship on her first return voyage from Sydney. On reaching England, Uncle William complained to the shipping company about the vessel's list, saying that he had to stand at the far corner of the bathroom to take a shower. The company took no notice of his complaint – and on her next trip out the *Waratah* disappeared without trace between Cape Town and Australia.

Young William Bragg wanted to try for a scholarship at Trinity College, Cambridge, but when he got to Trinity to take the exam he developed acute pneumonia. I went to see him, and found him sitting up panting for breath, with blue lips that I knew later to be characteristic of lobar pneumonia. He had a temperature in the region of 105° F and was coughing horribly and spitting blood. He took the scholarship examination in this state, with an invigilator in the room. With a brain like his father's he won the scholarship, and went up to Trinity. In 1910 it was decided that I should go to Gresham's School at Holt partly because it was a modern school with an interest in the latest scientific subjects, and partly because the train fare to Holt was cheap. Even so the fees worked out at the colossal sum of £100 a year. My brother had gone to Oundle, which was rather more expensive, but he had been left a small legacy by the actress Julia Cahill which was used for his education. But I had no legacy, and my schooling required very real sacrifice from my parents. Gresham's was a happy choice. The art master, whose name was Vivian Smith, was outstandingly good both for me and to me. At the very first drawing lesson he asked if I would like to join his special art class held in the classroom in winter and at outside sketching parties in the summer. Vivian Smith was a most attractive man, good at all games, and popular alike with the boys and other masters. Tragically, he was killed in the First World War, near the Somme. He had been on a night patrol between the lines, met an enemy patrol, and a fierce little battle ensued. His sergeant was wounded and, true to form, Smith went back to recover him under heavy enemy fire, at the cost of his own life.

In 1912 my mother's brother, Uncle Charlie Todd, who was a doctor in Adelaide, came to England and visited me at Gresham's. He turned up at precisely the right moment, for I was captaining my house at cricket, batting at the time and I made 50 runs! (A feat which I have not repeated since!) He stayed with my housemaster, J R Eccles, and after dinner that night he suggested that as he had no sons of his own, I might like to read medicine at Cambridge and succeed him in his practice in Adelaide. He promised me financial support if I needed it. When I said good bye to Uncle Charlie, walking from the dining room to my study, he pressed a gold sovereign into my hand. From then onwards I made up my mind to take up medicine - but as things turned out, it was not to be with Uncle Charlie.

In the summer term of 1913 I went up to Cambridge with several boys from the school to take the Little-Go. In those days, if you wanted your son to go to Cambridge you just wrote to the Master of the college concerned informing him that your son would be coming.

That first day at Caius College, Cambridge in October 1913 seemed overpowering and unfriendly compared with the security of Gresham's, but at dinner in Hall that evening a kindly undergraduate, Bob Niccol, came round to question the new intake about their athletic abilities. My only distinction was a second in the long jump at Gresham's, but I was duly told to attend for the Freshers' Sports at Fenners Ground. While at Cambridge I jumped 18 ft 10 ins, but all our efforts were eclipsed by an Australian called "The Twopenny" who jumped 22 ft. He, alas, was also killed in the 1914-18 war.

My family was still finding it difficult to make ends meet and when I went up to Cambridge my father said that he could afford to give me only half a crown a week for spending money. That was all right at home, but living as an undergraduate made things very difficult. However, I had an uncle, Arthur Tuffield, who had a son who wanted coaching in mathematics, and my uncle offered me two shillings an hour for coaching his son and two other boys. This added source of income enabled me to meet my commitments.

Soon after going up, I had joined the Special Reserve Cavalry, then called the "King's Colonial", but later known as King Edward's Horse. This was a sort of territorial army unit in which the horses as well as the men were civilians. The horses would be engaged during the week in pulling trams, cabs, carriages, bakers' carts, etc. and then at weekends they would go on parade. We were told that if we wished to continue with King Edward's Horse we should have to sign a piece of paper declaring that we would be willing to serve with the regiment overseas in the event of war. We did this willingly, little realising that in a year's time we would be in the trenches in Northern France.

In July 1914 we were in camp with King Edward's Horse at Canterbury, having taken our horses from Cambridge by train. On 4 August 1914 we were on parade as usual in Canterbury when the C.O. announced that war had been declared between England and Germany. He added that there would be no more parades that day, but told us to report as usual in the morning. Our immediate reaction was to go to the canteen and order pints of beer. After my second pint of beer I rushed out of the canteen shouting, "Where's that bloody Kaiser?"

# Chapter 2

# World War I

Next day I received a telegram from my Father saying "Sign nothing with regard to war service until you consult me." I had failed to mention that some nine months previously I had sold my body for £5 by signing a statement that I would serve overseas with King Edward's Horse in the event of war.

We stayed on at Canterbury for the next three weeks, full of excitement at the possibility of going out to France to have a go at the Boche. During this time all our horses from Cambridge were taken from us and sent to various cavalry depots to be shipped abroad and we were given instructions to scour the Canterbury area for more horses. We would find out where horses were to be seen, then about twelve of us, under the command of a sergeant, would be detailed to turn up with our bridles to requisition them. This was a sad job. We would arrive at a farm, and the owner would know only too well why we had come. Then there would be the sad parting as we rode the farmer's favourite hunter down his drive, with his wife and children in floods of tears, suddenly understanding the reality of war.

From Canterbury we went to Alexandra Palace on the outskirts of North London. The Palace was a huge Victorian exhibition hall which had been requisitioned, and we slept on straw palliasses on the floor. We went on collecting horses from the countryside in the same way, leaving London early in the morning by train and then riding the horses back to the Alexandra Palace. It was a point of honour to ride bareback and this was a considerable task, for these were country horses, quite unaccustomed to London traffic. At times, when we had a lot of horses to collect, we would be riding one and leading one on either side. Sometimes the sight of a tram coming down the middle of the road was too much - the horses would rear up and the led animals would break loose, to disappear down side alleys.

Surrounding Alexandra Palace there was a racecourse, and all our horses were tethered near the course, linked to a rope about one hundred yards long by means of a head collar alone. One night, when we had about 500 horses, all straight from the country and all highly nervous, something happened to stampede them. We never found out just what had happened, but they all broke loose, got on to the racecourse, and galloped hell for leather over it. Round about midnight they found an exit from the course along a narrow lane which had a steep drop on to the main road. The leading horses tried to stop, but the following horses surged on. Some tried to jump a thick hedge on to the road, and those that attempted this mostly broke their legs. Others were stopped by the mass of fallen animals.

It was a dreadful situation, pitch dark, with horses screaming and thrashing about wildly in the darkness. Our officers shouted, "Take a bridle chaps, and every man to a horse." We did our best, but it was not until about 4 a.m. that we had the situation under control. About 30 horses were dead, or had to be shot. After this we hobbled as many of our horses as we could, and indented urgently for a further supply of hobbles.

We shared our accommodation at Alexandra Palace with the Oxford, Cambridge, London and Liverpool squadrons of King Edward's Horse, and as soon as we all had a horse in from the country we set about schooling them. The Government had sensibly said that each trooper might choose his own horse, which he would look after completely, and eventually take into action in France. The most suitable type of horse was someone's favourite hunter, lovingly cared for, and used to picking its way over rough ground and carrying its master safely home. I chose a beautiful 17 hand bay, with a comfortable back which I had ridden up from the country, calling him Kaiser, much to the amusement of my colonel. Everyone liked Kaiser and in the evening when he was tethered in the lines, I would whistle to him and he would answer with a neigh. I never went to bed without saying goodnight to him, giving him a titbit of a sugar lump or an apple pinched from the canteen.

If one's horse was unsuitable for some reason, one was able to indent for a remount. There was a Remount Depot, which would take one's own unsuitable horse and either supply another in exchange, or tell you where to go in the country to collect one. Horses judged unfit for cavalry work would be sent to some less exacting job, to pull supply wagons, or to serve as packhorses.

When my father was working on the farm in his childhood his uncle often used to go to the horse sales at Newmarket. There, one could often pick up bargains – horses which were below racing standard but thoroughly good hacking horses. My great uncle used to come home in the evening and say to my father "Picked up a nice bit of blood in the sales at Newmarket today. Would you mind riding a couple of horses home tomorrow from Newmarket?" This was how my father developed his interest in riding, and made him keen to see that I had riding lessons in my young days. Those riding lessons were far removed from the contact with horses which we had in the army.

From the time war was declared we were paid at the standard rate of a cavalry trooper – one shilling a day and one penny extra for looking after the horse. And looking after the horse meant at least three hours a day of grooming, watering, and stable fatigue. By the end of each day we felt we had earned our penny! Another thing the army imposed on us: we were not allowed to grow beards, but there was a strict rule in the regiment that no one should shave his upper lip. We were told that this was to ensure a frightening appearance – the idea being that an enemy seeing a cavalry charge of men with handlebar moustaches bearing down on them would be so terrified that they would flee before we even got to them!

After about three weeks at the Alexandra Palace we were drafted down to Watford to continue our training. We spent one night on the way down setting up camp alongside a canal. During that night we had another disaster. We had no tents and had to sleep in the open in improvised sleeping bags – big sacks half-filled with straw. I woke up in the middle of the night to see the bellies of horses racing above me. We had left the horses tethered near the canal so that we should not have to fetch water for them in the morning, but a steam-driven barge on the canal startled them with its siren, and they stampeded. Once again Kaiser kept his head, and we caught up with them in a field about a mile away. We lost about four or five horses this time, bad enough, but not so bad as that dreadful night at the Alexandra Palace.

From October 19 until well into December our troop of about thirty men was billeted on Gammon's farm at Watford. If one was lucky one found a barn, but otherwise we were out in the open. Once a week it was our turn to do the cooking and on the night before we would go foraging for wood. If the weather was damp we would push the sticks down the tops of our trousers to dry them by the warmth of our bodies so that we could have fuel to light the fire for breakfast. To this day I can feel the discomfort of turning over at night to find twigs striking into my stomach.

Our days were spent schooling the horses, and practising over improvised jumps. I took the Army Rough Riding course while I was at Gammon's farm. I had had only my elementary riding lessons at Cambridge before going into King Edward's Horse, and found the Rough Riding course very tough. We had to jump horses while leading a horse on either side, and we had to be able to vault onto horses while they cantered by, running at them and putting the palm of one hand on the horse's withers. Another exercise was called "Mounted wrestling", when we had to canter bareback at our opposite number and try and pull him off. This, of course, helped to develop your knee grip.

On active service a cavalry section of four men, under the leadership of a lance corporal, might often want to dismount and continue a patrol on foot. This meant that the horses would have to be led away under cover. So one of our exercises consisted of riding one horse while leading two on one side and one on the other, looking for cover.

All this built up excitement as well as physical fitness, and we felt if only they would let us get out there we would soon show the Germans what an Englishman was made of. While we were at Watford the newspapers were full of the story of the Angels at Mons. The British and French were retreating under heavy attack and camped for the night. That night in the British camp a choir could be heard singing, and the troops were convinced they could see angels flying in the sky. This they interpreted as a sure sign that the Lord was on their side, and the next day fought back so vigorously that the Germans retreated. I can remember our thoughts at that time as a mixture of excitement that our troops were doing their stuff, and disappointment that we not be out there because the war would be over so quickly! Little did we know what was in store for us – four years of blood and sweat.

The first week at Gammon's farm it was my turn for cooking duty. I had never done anything more than boil an egg so it was with some anxiety that I embarked on my week as cook. The ration for a trooper in those days was one pound of meat per man per day, which seems colossal compared with the quantity of meat one has nowadays. My mates were fed up with endless stews, so I decided to have a change and make a steak and kidney pudding. I had no utensils, so went down to where the horses were tethered and took a bucket, cutting up the meat, vegetables and kidney into it. I then asked someone if he knew anything about pastry and was told the secret of adding suet and flour together. For a covering I tied a piece of sacking over the top of the bucket, after spreading out the pastry on top, and I tied the whole thing up with a piece of binder twine from the farm. The next problem was the actual cooking. I was told that this dish had to be boiled or steamed, so I took my bucket to the farmer's wife and asked if she would mind postponing her washing day and instead cook my steak and kidney pudding in her copper. This all proved very successful, but my pudding was so tough that there seemed to be more left afterwards than before anyone had started, and it kept us going most of the week.

One night when I was sharing night sentry duty with a man called Hanitsch watching the horses, the commanding officer came round. He asked me if I had seen the other sentry and when I said I had not, he went to look for him. Poor old Hanitsch was discovered in a grain bin where he had retired with a torch and a good book, but unfortunately fell asleep! He was at once put under arrest, his cap removed, and he was marched off for court martial. We were told that as this was a time of war the usual punishment for being asleep on sentry duty was death by firing squad. At the trial Hanitsch's advocate pleaded for leniency, and instead he was demoted to permanent sanitary orderly. The next time I saw Hanitsch was when one of my Bragg cousins was married in the twenties. I was asked to be an usher, and found to my astonishment that her bridegroom was none other than old Hanitsch.

We continued training keenly, and even had a jumping competition. The local boy scouts had been detailed to turn up to our camp each day to help us with our horse fatigues or by running small errands into Watford, and when we had to jump two to a horse, bareback, I chose a boy scout as my partner because of his light weight. This was a great advantage, and we won easily.

A great sorrow at Watford was that I had to part from Kaiser. I had been worried for some time about his soundness, for after a hard day's jumping he tended to go lame on his off-foreleg. My worst fears were confirmed when the camp vet certified him as unsound and to be returned to the remounts. It was one of the worst days of my life when I rode Kaiser over to the remounts depot at St Albans. I went with a friend from our unit, a colourful character called St Barbe Baker, who was later to win fame as the secretary of the Men of the Trees. I had known him in Cambridge. He was a tremendous talker, who helped to divert my thoughts on that sad journey, but, best of all, he had an aunt at St Albans who gave us both a good lunch – a great treat after our rough cooking in camp.

Soon after this came the final blow to King Edward's Horse. Just after Kitchener had been down to inspect us at Watford, we were told that the War Office had decided that cavalry charging with a sword was an outmoded form of offensive, chiefly because of the advent of the machine gun. This meant that in future the horse would be used only as a draught animal, or for lines of communication. Our King Edward's Horse was disbanded, and the troopers were invited to apply to join either the regular infantry, the gunners, or, in special cases, the Royal Horse Artillery. Bob Bragg, my cousin, who was in King Edward's Horse with me, joined the gunners. I, chiefly because of my success with the boy scout at the jumping competition, was accepted into the Royal Horse Artillery.

Bob went off first. He had to go on foot, which meant carrying his bedroll to the station, so I offered to take it for him on my horse. We set off together, Bob walking, and the bedroll on the horse, but we had not gone far when a taxi hurtled round the corner in the middle of the road hitting my horse fair and square in the chest, and throwing it back on its haunches, severely injured. The horse was sent back to remounts and I was sent to the C.O. for a severe reprimand. That was the last time I ever saw Bob Bragg – a great friend and a fine person. Soon after joining his battery he was sent to the Dardanelles, where he was wounded in the thigh by a Turkish shell. Gas gangrene set in, and his leg was amputated at a field hospital but he died before he could be got back to a base hospital. I was in France by then, and my father, knowing how close I had been to Bob, tried to have the news of his death kept from me, but I had already learned of it from other sources.

I got my posting to Woolwich on 20 December 1914 and was so excited that I went straight to Woolwich from Watford without going home for Christmas (in case the War Office should suddenly change its mind!). I was to be commissioned into the Royal Horse Artillery, so my status at Woolwich was that of an officer-cadet. This gave me a room with a servant – a change indeed from the tough, open life to which I had grown accustomed. When we wanted a horse at Woolwich we would merely tell our man to have it ready at a given time. This was very nice in some ways, but in fact I missed the horse-fatigues and grooming which had made us, as troopers, grow so close to our horses.

At night we attended the Mess, where there would be a fearsome array of the old school of distinguished officers, with their Boer War medals displayed on their uniforms. I don't think they were so impressed with us – indeed, they told us that we must realise our position, and that we were only temporary gentlemen as it was a time of war.

Some of the men who had enrolled with me had seen very little in the way of riding-school, and the gruelling Rough Riding course which I had been through at Watford made me seem quite an expert, so I was chosen to lead the church parade. I am afraid that this led to my making a sad mistake. A mounted officer always salutes with the right hand, but a trooper salutes with the hand on the opposite side to which he is paired by his officer. When I was paired by my senior on the church parade I saluted with my left hand because he had paired me on the right, forgetting that I was no longer the trooper of two days ago. It is strange to think how little things like this remain so important in memory.

I duly passed out at Woolwich and was commissioned into the R.H.A. I had never been abroad before, so I felt tremendous excitement when I had orders to take 120 men as reserves to a transit camp at Honfleur, near Le Havre, with a fellow officer. We arrived at Southampton in the train with our men and ordered them out of the train to fall in on the platform. I took the precaution of going through the train to make sure that nothing had been left behind, and was horrified to discover two rifles amongst all the newspapers and bits of orange peel with which the train was littered. When I got back to my party I found two gormless young soldiers standing to attention in the ranks, still unaware that they had left their rifles behind and would have to face the enemy with their bare hands!

On the crossing, we officers were ordered to post sentries round the ship to watch for German submarines – if a periscope was seen, they were to open fire with rifles. Fortunately, we crossed the Channel without meeting any submarines, and made our way safely to the camp at Honfleur. It was a dreadful feeling to leave our men there, knowing that most of them would probably be dead in a few weeks. We had to stay the night in Le Havre, and spent the evening in a cafe where there were a lot of soldiers en route to and from England with the local girls hanging around. This was my first taste of French high life – at its lowest level.

In May 1915 I saw my name at last on the notice board to report to Tidworth for overseas service. Our horses belonged to Woolwich, so we had to leave them behind, collecting fresh ones from the Kitchener Division at Tidworth.

We lived in tents at Tidworth Pennings and were attached to the 37th Division. So rapid was the rate of change of men arriving and departing that soon after I got to the Division there was a sudden lack of commanding officers. As I had been commissioned for two weeks longer than anyone else there, I was made acting divisional commander for three days, theoretically with about 20,000 men under my command – a position I have never equalled since. The new divisional commander soon came down and put me in my place.

Life was pretty comfortable at Tidworth Pennings. My pay was two shillings a day, and I was provided with two horses, a groom and a servant. One horse which I chose from the depot was a beautiful black mare which had slightly "gone in the wind", but she was a thoroughbred and a joy to ride, with perfect action, as long as one did not want to race her. I called her Maria. The other was an Argentine bright bay gelding which I called Betsey Jane. This horse did not have the quality of Maria, but was very handsome. Once when I was riding Maria on manoeuvres at the firing range, the Brigade Major came over to me and said that my horse was of too high a quality for my junior rank, so would I please return her to the depot and choose one more suitable for my position. I hastily explained that she had gone in the wind, and so was able to keep my precious Maria.

Also at Tidworth was my old art master from Gresham's, Vivian Smith, who had volunteered for service. There was no conscription in England until 1916 and he, like many others, had been fired by the thought that his country needed him. It was good to have dinner with him in the Mess, talking over more pleasant topics than the war.

In July 1915, while I was at Tidworth my mother and sister Alice came down to see me. I had booked rooms for them in a pub so that they could stay the weekend, and that very weekend I got my posting to an unknown destination in France. We spent Sunday having a very peaceful picnic and next day I boarded the troop train for Southampton. The horses travelled in cattle trucks attached to the train.

My mother and sister came to see me off. I was excited at the thought that at last the time to prove myself had come, but for my mother and Alice it was a sad departure. I can see them now, standing in a big field to the left of the station as we filed into the train.

Chapter 3

# Embarkation for the Western Front and Wounded

All the horses climbed up the gangplank onto the cross-channel boat except for Maria. She refused completely, nearly falling into Southampton harbour in her struggles to defeat the efforts of the crew to persuade her to go on board. Finally, a sling was put under her belly and she was hoisted into the hold of the ship by crane. Luckily we had a smooth crossing, for horses, unlike humans, are unable to be sick, and suffer greatly in rough weather.

On disembarking we set off on the 100 mile journey to the front. We were an impressive cavalcade of gunners with their guns, ammunition waggons and RASC supply waggons, all horse drawn. In these motorised days it is hard to convey how important the horse was then: there was virtually no motor transport, except an occasional ambulance and motor cyclist dispatch rider. Our guns were hitched to the ammunition waggons, pulled by teams of six horses. When the guns went into action they, and their accompanying ammunition waggons, would be brought up into position by the horses. Then the waggons would be lined up alongside the guns, and the drivers would unhitch the horses and take them behind the lines for cover.

The weather for our march to the front was wonderfully fine

and the nights warm, which was pleasant for us because we spent the nights in the open, rolled up in ground sheets with our two standard-issue army blankets. We always slept close to our horses, which were tethered to a long rope in the usual manner, and hobbled for safety. My thoughts on that 100 mile march were chiefly of anxiety about whether I could really stand up to the strain of fighting, and face the enemy when the time came.

As we drew near the front we could hear the heavy guns getting closer and closer. We had been ordered to join the Canadians at the front line, between Ypres and Armentières at a place called Ploeg Street, where the fighting was very hot. On the day we arrived the officers only - three subalterns, a captain and a major -went into the trenches to have a look at a mine which was going to be exploded. On the way we passed a burial party – there was the corpse of a young soldier wrapped up on the ground, a padre, and two soldiers who had just finished digging the grave. As we passed, a shell came over, and landed quite nearby. The padre and the grave-diggers jumped into the grave for safety, leaving the corpse which could be hurt no more, outside.

The line had been stationary for some months in a situation approaching stalemate. It was considered good for the morale of the troops to have frequent raiding parties at night, storming enemy lines and returning in the early hours of the morning with several men lost and no ground won.

Our guns were dug into pits behind the infantry line and trained on the enemy. As officers, we had to take it in turns to spend two nights at a stretch up in the front, to direct fire. This entailed going into the trenches in the evening, and when it was properly dark crawling between the lines, so that one would get a good view in the morning of the enemy's wire. We had with us a field telephone and operator, and we used to spend part of the night digging a shallow bunker to give us cover in the morning. When daylight came we would direct fire, via the field telephone, on movement of enemy troops, or, if there was no sign of movement, on to the wire. Much of our work then was concerned with trying to cut the enemy's wire. We would direct the first rounds a little high, so that they would land beyond the wire, and the next a trifle short, thus bracketing the target. When we had found the true range we would send back a message requesting fire at one round per minute. Our guns would then continue firing at this rate for perhaps 300 rounds, smashing the wire and making an entrance for the next night's raiding party.

On one occasion I had just given the order "Continue at one minute", when one of our own shells landed only a few yards away from us, cutting our telephone wire. It was a frightening situation, for our guns had clearly mistaken the range, and I could not countermand the order to continue firing because our telephone line was cut. If we stayed in the crater where we were lying we were bound to be hit eventually; if we moved out, we were likely to be shot by an enemy sniper. We were saved by the telephonist, who gallantly crawled out, found the broken telephone wire, and managed to reconnect it. This enabled me to send back a message redirecting the fire.

We quickly became skilled at estimating the fall of shells, both our own and the enemy's, by observing their trajectory, and listening to the whistle as a shell approached. Particularly with howitzers, the pitch of the whistle gave a good indication of how near a shell was likely to land.

With the approach of autumn the rains came, and the mud over the whole front became indescribably horrible. It was not until the next year (1916) that duckboards were issued – these brought about a big improvement. There were rats everywhere; a rat even climbed into the top of my sleeping bag while I was asleep, and I woke to find it gnawing at a comb in my pocket. Everybody suffered from "Trench Feet", which made moving around agony. "Trench Foot" was basically caused by frostbite, which first affected the tissues, and then constant wet feet, boots, socks and putties would promote secondary infection to produce a chronic condition that was miserably painful.

Our food at times was not too bad. Once a month we had a gift hamper from Fortnum and Mason's which contained a cake, biscuits, and a small bottle of whisky. We had a tot either of our own whisky or of issue rum each night, with a double tot after our two day stint in the forward observation post. When we were up in the front we had to scrounge what we could from the infantry colonel; if we were unlucky in our scrounging we had to survive on a tin of bully beef and dog biscuits (as we called them).

A bitter aspect of life at the front in that First World War was the treatment meted out to so-called "cowards". Some men cannot stand the strain to which soldiers on active service are liable to be subjected, and in the Second World War this was recognised, and treated much more leniently. In 1914-18, however, the penalty for an utterly broken nerve could be death.

*Tidd with my horse*

I remember vividly one poor chap who could not face the enemy, and who was duly court-martialled. He was given a bottle of whisky overnight and shot at dawn next morning, supposedly as an example to the rest of us. I doubt if such harsh discipline had any effect except to make men who really understood the suffering of the front feel hateful and resentful of the brasshats who imposed the punishment.

In May 1916 I was given a week's leave. This was a great excitement. I saw many of my friends who had continued their medical studies at Cambridge, and I couldn't help thinking what soft lives they had compared with my last two years. Conscription was not introduced until near the end of 1916, and in the early part of the war the army was so concerned about the heavy casualties among doctors that medical students were encouraged to stay at home and qualify. The system in those early days was for army doctors to attend the wounded in the front line. This led to such heavy casualties that at one time it was feared that the whole nation would begin to run out of doctors. Later the system was changed, with the aim of getting the wounded as quickly as possible to field hospitals. This gave seriously wounded men a better chance of recovery than could have been given by treatment at the front, and it also saved many medical lives.

When I got back to the front after my leave I developed a sore throat. At first I tried to ignore it, but when I turned yellow all over and began passing urine that was almost black I had to report sick. Infective hepatitis was diagnosed, and I was sent back to the base hospital on the west coast. After treatment I was transferred to Ensley House hospital in Marylebone. When I got better I had a couple of weeks convalescence at home, and was then posted back to the front.

My C.O. had particularly asked if I could be posted back to the same regiment. My servant Tidd came up to meet me when I landed in France, and we cadged a lift on a RASC supply wagon pulled by four horses. We were given an address in a village where, we were told, we could stay for the night – it was one on a list of houses which could be requisitioned for temporary accommodation. When we got there we found an old woman in bed in the room we were supposed to occupy. She was very cross at being disturbed, but she got out of bed and, to

*Self in World War 1 with a friend*

*In the Western front with a friend*

show her feelings for us, she reached under the bed for a chamber-pot and used it in front of us - not even war had prepared me for anything like this! Then the old woman put the full chamber-pot on a chair beside the bed, and marched off downstairs. In spite of all this I went to sleep quickly enough. Tidd, who said he could sleep anywhere, went downstairs and slept on the kitchen table.

Tidd was a loyal, faithful friend through all my time in France. He was 47 years old, had been servant to a general in the Boer War, and was a real old campaigner. During my brief spell as Divisional Commander at Tidworth I had to select a servant and I had looked through the references of all the various soldiers who wished to be officers' servants, Tidd's character appealed to me. He had ten children at home and he said that when the war was over he was good for another ten. After our night in the old woman's house Tidd came upstairs and asked "Anything you want sir?" "What would you say, Tidd, if I asked you to get me some milk?" I replied. "I would get it for you," said Tidd. "But you can't speak French," I said. "I know I can't, but I would go to a farm and say 'Dulay' to whoever opened the door." He went off, and sure enough he returned about half an hour later bringing milk for me.

In the spring of 1916 we moved south, farther down the line on the Somme. We were stationed outside a small village called Englebelmer where we positioned our guns. Things were hotting up for the battle of the Somme. Our line had a ridge in front of it called Mary Redan, and it was here that I encountered the practice of mining. The Sappers had nearly finished a mine-tunnel deep below the level of the enemy lines, running about 200 yards under their line. This was partly propped, partly left just plain earth, and it took about 20 minutes to crawl through. The first time I went along the shaft the thing which amazed me was hearing the Germans digging a shaft in the opposite direction, frantically trying to finish theirs and blow up our lines before we were able to set off our charge. We felt quite safe as long as we could hear the Germans digging, as they would not blow up their own men. But when the digging stopped, anxiety mounted. For this reason we had a trooper placed at the farther end of the shaft, and told him to telephone if the digging on the German side ceased. The day I went up, there was a trooper sitting huddled up on an old box with a muffler round his face, reading the latest issue of home chat by candlelight.

The German tactics were to build very deep trenches to be safe from our gunfire, whereas we were told to dig shallow trenches, as it was considered that men would be more reluctant to get out of deep trenches for raiding parties. The analogy here, I suppose, was the fear of making one's bed too comfortable!

At the end of June 1916 we shelled the German lines unmercifully with everything we had to prepare for a big Allied offensive. On July 1 we blew our mine (our little trooper having been recalled, with his home chat) and our troops poured over the top. The technique was to blow a mine and then run for the crater which formed cover. This time, however, the Germans were quicker than we were, as they had suspected our mine, and had been ready for it. When our troops reached the crater they found it already occupied, and the Germans coming out of their own trenches with machine guns. Our casualties in that offensive were appalling – out of some 2,300 men who took part in the attack, about 1,500 were killed on the first day. Casualties in the Second World War were nothing like those dreadful figures on the Somme. One reads occasionally in newspapers of friends being killed on the roads, and such news is a horrible shock. On that first day of July 1916 fifteen hundred of the men with whom I had shared life at Cambridge, Canterbury, the Alexandra Palace, Watford, Woolwich and Salisbury Plain were killed. That is a memory from which one never wholly recovers.

As a reward for our gallant work in the Somme offensive we were drafted down the line to Ypres, where we were told the action was less hot. There was a dreadful stench of rotting horse and human flesh as we marched into Ypres.

The RASC had been ordered to send a supply waggon into Ypres with special rations for our men after their ordeal on the Somme. Just as the waggon turned up there was a gas warning. The crew, not being as accustomed as we were to the front, got the wind up and the last we saw of our precious goodies was the four-horse waggon galloping hell for leather away from Ypres. We spent all that day with our gas masks on. These were the old-issue masks which only worked when wet; so if there was no water available, we had to piddle into the top. Breathing all day long our urine warm was hellish, but I supposed it was better than gas.

While at Ypres I was sent on duty to the forward position – as I explained earlier, we used to make our way to these forward observation posts at night. Reconnoitring through my field glasses during the day I spotted a dead willow tree which, I thought, would make a good observation post. So that night I crawled into No Man's Land and the morning found me comfortably installed in my hollow tree with the occasional sniper's bullet thudding into the trunk. The Sappers thought my tree an excellent idea, but regarded it as a weakness that it might be knocked to pieces by bullets and shrapnel. So they made an imitation tree in painted metal, and crept out at night to saw down my tree and replace it with their metal replica. It was a reasonably secure observation post, but I never liked it as much as my old willow tree: every time a sniper's bullet hit there was a harsh clang instead of the soft thud of the bullet going into wood.

We stayed at Ypres until October 1916 and were then moved south to relieve the French who were finding it rather hot. I found myself in charge of my battery, as all my fellow officers were casualties – Major Hawkesley, Captain Stoney, and 1st Lieut. Drummond had been killed, and 2nd Lieut. Robinson had been wounded in the Ypres salient.

At the end of a day's march we met the French commander, who told me that he wanted me to go another 20 miles up to the front line, to assess the position and decide where the guns should be positioned. I therefore set out with my groom, picking my way through all the shell holes and barbed wire to meet the French guide who was going to show me the French forward position. We got there about 02.00, having covered the last few miles on foot. Then we lay up until we could survey the position in daylight. I made sketches of our position, marking all the relevant natural and enemy obstacles, so that I had a very clear picture of where everything was when my own guns arrived on the following night.

It was almost winter again, and the mud was horrible. Our gunners had developed a drill for pulling guns out of the mud. If one team got stuck, the driver of the following team would at once detach his horses and add them to the team that was stuck, making twelve horsepower. This usually got the gun out. When dawn came I was relieved to see that we had five of our six guns in position, whereas the other batteries had only two or three.

I was feeling quite exhausted after this effort, having had two nights without sleep. At last I crept into a room in an empty house, which had been shelled and half knocked down, and got into my sleeping bag. I had just got off to sleep when my subaltern came in to wake me. There was a horse down in the mud, he said, and would I come and shoot it? I made a supreme effort and went off with my revolver and shot it. I had just got to sleep again when the subaltern returned to tell me that they had found another horse in the dark, floundering hopelessly in the mud. I felt physically unable to go off again, so the subaltern said that he would shoot the beast himself, adding that he had

*Sister Alice in Uniform with a friend*

performed this melancholy task before. I explained very carefully how one had to be absolutely exact in calculating the point of entry of the bullet by drawing lines from the base of each ear to the opposite eye, placing the revolver where they crossed. He went off into the night, and when I woke the next morning I asked him how he had managed. To my distress, he said that the first bullet had not killed the horse, which had started jumping around, the pain making subsequent shots more difficult, but that it did eventually die. I have never forgiven myself for that act of weakness and weariness on my part and the needless suffering of that horse haunts me still. I remember my father saying to me before I left for the front, "Remember, old chap, a gentleman is never tired,"

That incident led me to develop a new technique for dealing with horses which had become so bogged down in mud that they could struggle no longer. I used to grab the horse's tongue so that it was unable to close its mouth, pull the tongue to one side and then pour about one third of a bottle of neat whisky down its throat. In about two minutes the fierce spirit stirred the horse to make a stupendous last effort to struggle free. After developing the whisky technique I never had to shoot another horse, and I was able to help many of my comrades' horses to their feet again.

We spent the winter of 1916/17 in the same section of the line, but in March 1917 we marched north to Arras. The town was dreadfully battered. We arrived in the middle of the night and were given a guide to help us place our guns in position before dawn. It was incredibly cold that night, and we were out in the open in trenches. Then it started snowing. When the morning came everything was covered in a carpet of white and in front of us was Vimy Ridge, occupied by the Germans. We were excellent targets with our white backing.

That evening they shelled our cookhouse. We heard a shell whistle overhead and then explode nearby – it sent a piece of shrapnel straight at our cook, Gunner Dunn. He was a cheerful cockney fellow, always looking on the bright side and never grumbling about all the hardships we endured together. That bit of shrapnel took a huge piece of skull out of the back of his head through which his brain could be seen slopping out. I can see him now, saying "I've had my chips – I'm for blighty," as he fell sideways, dead. How extraordinary, I thought, that someone could actually speak with so much brain damage.

I had had a letter from Cambridge that morning telling me that my sister Alice had joined the V.A.D, and was stationed at a base hospital at Boulogne. As this was only about 60 miles from Arras I thought I might be able to get a couple of days off and visit her. A friend in the regiment also had a sister nursing in that hospital, so we decided to ride over together. The horses would manage it, if we went carefully.

I rode Maria, and we set off early in the morning, trotting, with an occasional canter, making sure that whenever we came to a watering place the horses had a short drink – mouthfuls only. There is nothing that exhausts a horse more than trying to make it work on a belly full of water, but the horses did not like being taken away from water before they had finished drinking all that they felt they wanted. It was a wonderful crisp March day, a far cry from a few nights before when the snow fell.

We reached Boulogne at about 17.30 that evening, and had a wonderful evening exchanging home news and taking the girls out to a meal in the hotel. The next morning we set off early back to Arras, again taking great care of our horses as we realised how dependent we were on them. After this trip Alice wrote a curious letter back to Cambridge, saying that she had had a premonition that she would see her brother again soon.

On 5 April 1917 – just before the battle of Arras – I had to go between the lines on a forward reconnaissance trip with my signaller. The distance between the two lines was about two miles at this point, but, because of Vimy Ridge, the enemy could see our position very well. We set off when it was still dark, about six o'clock in the morning, hoping to get dug into a position before dawn broke. Because of the distance between the lines we had to carry a huge roll of wire, so our progress was considerably slowed. We had not quite reached the site where we had planned to hide up for the day when the enemy spotted us. Shell after shell came over in our direction, all round us. Suddenly I heard a howitzer shell coming over with a sinister note, and I shouted to my signaller to get down. I pushed him and the roll of wire into a disused trench, which was close by us.

The shell landed virtually at my feet, but luckily most of the blast went upwards. All the same I was caught all down one side by a shower of shrapnel and the blast lifted me bodily, hurling me into the air, and I landed in a crumpled heap alongside my signaller in the trench. It is impossible to describe to anyone who has never been blasted the extraordinary feeling the only thing I can say is that it must be much like being run over by a steamroller. One's whole body feels numbed and tingling, and not really part of oneself.

When I came to my senses I inspected the wounds, and the signaller telephoned to the C.O. to report the state of affairs. It was impossible to bring out a stretcher, so I had to struggle with an arm on my signaller to get back to the lines 1½ miles away. What an immense distance it seemed! When, eventually I reached the lines I was told to go ¾ mile further into Arras, where the Field First Aid Post was situated. The town square at Arras was an extraordinary sight. The First Aid Post was an old brewery, which had been requisitioned, but there was no room left in the cellars and there were men with varying degrees of wounds lying all over the pavements and roadway. The shot of morphia which the C.O. had promised me on arrival seemed far away as I lay on the kerb, exhausted by the effort of walking. Tidd sat beside me, trying to keep me cheerful with his optimistic chatter – saying that he would not mind some nice wounds like that to get him back to Blighty!

I waited from about 11 a.m. until 5 o'clock that evening, when some transport was available and I was told that I was to be transferred to a Casualty Clearing Station by ambulance. There were several of us crowded into that ambulance. I can still picture those last moments of my three years on the Western Front. There were tears in both our eyes as I said good-bye to the faithful Tidd. The town square of Arras grew smaller and smaller as we drove away from it, and the smoke over the battlefront turned hazy in the distance. The relief of leaving that hell counteracted the intense pain down my left side from those wonderful wounds which were enabling me to go away from the front honourably.

Chapter 4

# Invalided Back Home

In Boulogne Hospital Alice was taking a breakfast tray up to a patient when she was told that her brother had been wounded and was in the Casualty Clearing Station. Her mind went blank and she let go of the tray and was left standing in the middle of the ward, with broken crockery at her feet.

But I had not yet got to hospital. The Casualty Clearing Station was some distance from Boulogne, and I was taken first to the operating theatre there to have my wounds tidied up. There were four tables in the theatre with one anaesthetist to direct the administration of open ether, while four surgeons worked. One large piece of shrapnel was removed from my elbow quite easily, but several other pieces deep in my thigh could not be found. There were no antibiotics then, and, as was feared, in a few days when the bacteria had had a little time to get established and multiply I started to run a high fever. I was looked after by a nurse of about 40, who had been a District Nurse before the war in England. She had a son in the front line, of whom she said I reminded her, and she lavished on me all her maternal affection.

But this was only a clearing station, and it was soon time for me to be moved on to Boulogne. I asked particularly if I could be sent to the Seventh Stationary Hospital, where Alice was working, and, after a lot of persuasion, I was told that this would be done. I was therefore put on the train for Boulogne still with my fever, and with a label pinned on my sleeve giving my name and destination at the Seventh Stationary Hospital.

My fever continued in hospital. Often my temperature would soar to 105°F and my thigh would become huge and throbbing. On one ward round I heard the surgeon discussing with a junior the possibility of gas in my leg. Gas gangrene is caused by a particularly virulent bacterium called Clostridium Welchi which, like its fellow Clostridium Tetani, spreads through tissue with terrifying rapidity, producing bubbles of carbon dioxide and thriving in conditions where the wound has no contact with the air. A deep puncture wound is an almost ideal condition for gas gangrene.

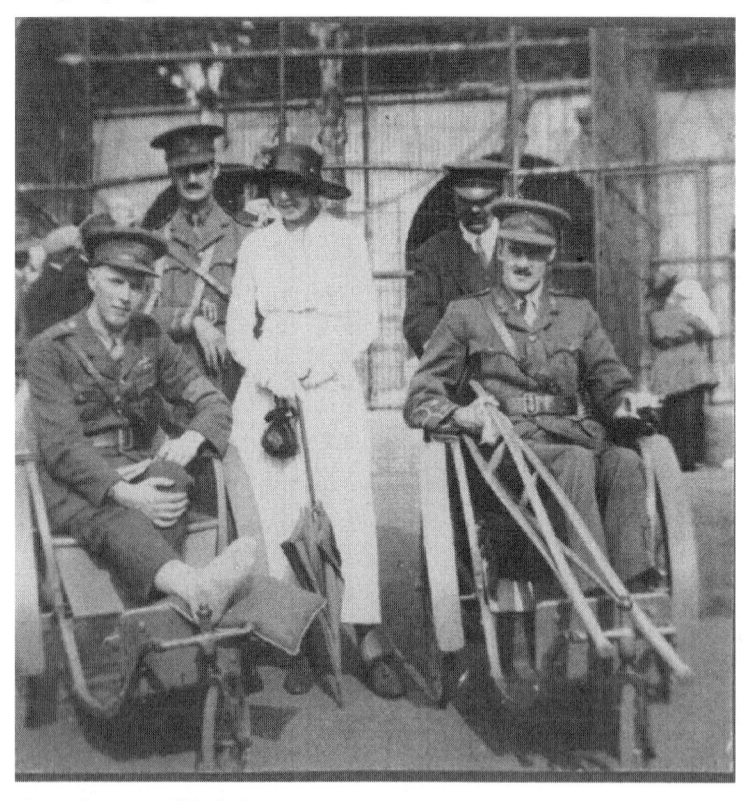

*Convalescing in 'blighty'*

Hearing the surgeon talking about the possibility of gas in my thigh put the wind up me; I remembered only too well the fate of my cousin Bob Bragg, who died when they tried to amputate his leg. I was still more alarmed when I was told by the night sister that I was to be taken down to the theatre for another operation. The relief when I woke in the morning and found that I still had my leg is indescribable – the operation had been to insert ten drainage tubes into my thigh to remove pus.

My condition became less critical and I was considered fit to be sent back to hospital in England. We landed at Dover and went up to Charing Cross by train. It was a hysterical scene there. Inside the station there were queues of white ambulances, and crowds of young girls with bunches of flowers, cheering and throwing the flowers and kisses as the stretchers were taken out of the train. A friend of Alice's, Capt McIntosh, had arranged for me to go to Carlton House Terrace where Lady Risley had opened up her house as a hospital. It had balconies overlooking the Mall, and was still full of the splendour and luxury of pre-war years.

Nowadays when a nurse does a dressing she uses nothing but sterile instruments. In those days, however, the nurse used to come down the ward dressing our wounds from the same trolley seven days a week, so that if one patient developed a particularly nasty bacterium, in a few days we all had it. The resident surgeon was Dr James Wyatt, who was later to be an obstetrician at St Thomas's Hospital and he eventually plugged the wound with Savoy Nigra.

The last stage of my convalescence was spent at Chichester Terrace, Brighton. Morale was improved down there, and we must have looked a fine sight in wheelchairs or hobbling along the front. Walking out with my crutches one evening I met a nice young woman, who helped me along. I asked her if she would like to come for a walk with me, and whether she would like to go to the beach to hear the waves break. "No," she said, "don't fancy the beach "cos all them pebbles stick into yer back."

Every day I used to go down to the sea and bathe my wounds in salt water I am sure this contributed more than anything to their improvement.

By Christmas 1917-18 I was home at Cambridge. Alice was at home, too, as she was convalescing after diphtheria, so we had a grand and happy reunion.

As I recovered from my wounds there was a suggestion that I should join Uncle Will in his experiments for plotting the position of enemy guns by an early form of radio location. I was not keen on this, for I knew that I should be hopelessly out of my depth; and the news that Uncle Will and Cousin Willie had just been awarded a Nobel Prize confirmed my feelings. I therefore attended an Army Medical Board to determine whether I was fit to be sent back to the Front. I felt that after nearly four years I had done my bit, and it was a great relief when I was classified as unfit for overseas service. I was sent instead to an Ordnance Depot outside Chelmsford.

We had a very relaxed time there, and we spent hours in the local pub. I had a good horse, and hunted whenever I could. This annoyed the adjutant, who disliked hunting. Learning that I proposed to attend a meet in one of the nearby villages, the adjutant selected the day of the meet for an inspection by our colonel – Colonel Schofield. I was not so timid then as I once was, and I was not going to miss a good meet. As I rode out of camp Col. Schofield rode in, "everyone present?" "Yes sir, everyone except Captain Squires, and I can't get in touch with him." "I should think not," said the Colonel. "I passed him on the way into camp, and he looked as though he was riding out to the meet. Jolly good show. Damn fine sport hunting. Should be encouraged - next best thing to military action."

I had not been long at Chelmsford when I received a letter from the War Office saying that anyone who had started medical studies before the war could be released from the army to continue medical training. This was to make up for the vast numbers of doctors who had been killed on active service.

# Chapter 5

# St Thomas's Hospital

So in May 1918 I returned to Cambridge. It was a strange feeling to walk through the same gates that I had entered not long before as a timid little boy from Gresham's – what an unbelievable difference those years on the Western Front had made!

I worked hard at anatomy and physiology to pass my Second BA in one term, but I was very short of money. My main asset was £250 – the maximum of wound gratuity, known as "blood money". My father had no spare money to let me have, and I became very anxious about what to do when my gratuity ran out. I had banked on having Uncle Charlie's financial help in order to qualify; this was not now available. So I went to see Uncle Will, and he said that he would apply to the Ex-Officers' Benevolent Fund, which was set up to help officers whose education had been interfered with by the war. The Fund generously gave me £100 a year for three years, which I could draw in quarterly instalments. It was this money which enabled me to qualify.

There was a sharp division at Cambridge then between those who had been to the Front and those who had not. Those of us who had come from the Front met fairly regularly at a club which we called The Duds – that is to say, something which had been thrown at the enemy and failed to explode! Our patron was George Robey, the famous comedian, and as I was the secretary of the club I often found myself writing to him. We did not see much of him in person because he had so many engagements, but he always took the trouble to send a message conveying his good wishes for anything we did.

After passing my Second MB examination that summer I went up to St Thomas's Hospital in the autumn of 1918. I lived in digs in Bayswater, kept by a Mrs. Watts – bed, breakfast and evening meal for £2 a week. I invested in a beautiful £10 Raleigh bicycle so that I should never have to use expensive public transport. I had many happy trips to Cambridge on that old bicycle, cycling down on a Saturday and back to London on Sunday.

On 11 November 1918 the war ended and London started its social life again. Hostesses were longing to give dances, and sometimes we would go to dances three nights in one week. All the girls would have programmes and I always felt that it was bad luck that some girls could get their programmes, filled up almost at once while others (often those who would make far better

*The staff at St. Thomas's Hospital
(I am centre at rear)*

*The ward St. Thomas's Hospital*

wives) would sit sadly alone with only the occasional name on their programmes. The girls we considered really caddish were those who would double or treble book their programmes, and then make some excuse not to dance if a more handsome fellow came along. I remember getting very cross with one girl whom I had booked for the second waltz. I saw her earlier dancing with some handsome fellow, but when my turn came she was nowhere to be seen. I spent the second waltz looking for her, and trying hard not to look as though I had lost anything. I strongly suspected that she was in a dark corner of the balcony with her former partner – shocking behaviour.

On the way back to St Thomas's early in the morning after one dance I was walking through Westminster with my friend Douglas McLean. We were not drunk, but, perhaps, slightly unsteady. Passing the Houses of Parliament, Douglas said, "There's a debate on. Let's go in and listen to it." We made our way into the Strangers' Gallery but had scarcely sat down when an attendant came along and said that we were making too much noise. If we did not leave at once, he added, he would call for force to throw us out. So we left, not quite understanding why he had been so upset.

When the time came for me to do midwifery at St Thomas's I had to leave my digs in Bayswater for lodgings nearer and I moved to new rooms in Lambeth Palace Road, sharing with a great friend, Kenneth Taliman. Soon after we moved in the landlady wanted to get us out, because she thought she could let the rooms to a student at Guy's Hospital, who would pay more. One evening Kenneth and I were going to a dance. Dressed in our tail coats, with silk hats on the sideboard, we sat in our mean little room to have our supper – a meagre helping of thin stew, followed by a slice of syrup tart. Still feeling hungry after this, I had a slice of bread and marmalade. I was eating this when the landlady came in.

"What's this I see? Stealing marmalade," she said fiercely, "I only provide two courses in the evening - marmalade's for breakfast. What's more, I don't cater for toffs. You can take a week's notice."

The champagne at the dance that night seemed doubly enjoyable. We moved next day a few doors down the road to the students' hostel, more familiarly known as "the brothel".

The obstetrician at St Thomas's then was Sir John Fairbourne, and a pleasing little story is told about him. He was walking over Westminster Bridge one day when he came across a crowd of people, policemen and a fire engine. Inquiring what had happened, he found that a small boy had pushed his head through the cast iron balustrade of the bridge, and he could not get it out. "But it's all right, Guv'nor," a bystander said. "We have sent for gas and acetylene to cut him free." Sir John walked closer to the lad and said, "Bend your head onto your chest." The boy did this and instantly offered a narrower diameter, which enabled him to withdraw his head easily. Everyone was impressed by this, asked Sir John how he had managed it. Observing "I earn my living by getting large heads through small spaces", he continued on his way across the bridge.

In those days I used to see a good deal of Lady Clancarty, who lived in Cadogan Gardens. Her husband was an Irish peer, about 30 years older than she was, who spent most of his time in Ireland. Lady Clancarty was a most attractive woman, and I used to escort her to dances and dinner parties given by her friends. She was holding a charity bazaar one Saturday, and had asked me to contribute to her sweet stall – I think expecting a guinea box of chocolates. I was still as impoverished as ever, so I turned up with two pennyworth of boiled sweets, which, I am glad to say, she took in the right spirit. One afternoon I was standing on the steps of her house in Cadogan Gardens when an immaculate old gentleman with a silk hat and a cane joined me. "Who are you waiting for?" he asked. "I've come to see Lady Clancarty," I answered. "The devil you have," he said and opened the door for me with a latchkey. We were given tea in the drawing room, not quite as informally as I was used to.

Financially I still had great difficulties, and they were suddenly made worse by another disaster in the family. My father's brother (with whom he had worked as a boy on the farm) had a son, Charlie Squires, who had been articled to my father and worked with him in his solicitor's practice. In 1919 my father retired, and the practice was taken over by a London firm of solicitors. They agreed to keep open the Cambridge branch as long as Charlie could manage it, paying my father a pension of £3 a week. It was further agreed, however, that if anything happened to Charlie Squires, I and my brother Stenie would have to guarantee the pension.

Driving back to Cambridge one foggy night on his motor-bicycle and sidecar, Charlie had a head-on collision with a lorry and died in Hitchin hospital. His wife, who was in the sidecar, was severely injured.

Charlie's death meant that the London solicitors were no longer under any obligation to pay my father's pension. I went to see my brother about this, and although it was difficult for both of us we agreed to find £1 10s a week each to provide the pension of £3. We pretended that this still came from the solicitors, and to the end of his life my father never knew that his pension was in fact provided by Stenie and me.

In March 1920, about a week before I was due to take my finals, a great friend, Harold Allen, invited me to stay with his family at Liverpool for the Grand National. His father, Sir John Sandeman Allen, lived in a large house called Princes Park; everything was lavish, with non-stop champagne and badges for all the races. That was the year that Jack Anthony won on Troytown.

I took the conjoint exam in order to qualify a few months earlier than waiting for the Cambridge examination, but I duly took the Cambridge exam as well a little later. My first job was Casualty Officer and Resident Anaesthetist at St Thomas's. It was very hard work, sometimes having to deal with accidents and operations all night through. We received no pay – it was considered an honour to be allowed to work at the hospital, but we were given free board and lodging, and free beer with our supper!

That Christmas we put on the usual amateur pantomime, combining with the students in a show that had many songs about the staff. Suddenly we were approached by a charity organisation and asked to do a performance at the Coliseum. This was quite frightening, particularly as King George V and Queen Mary were due to attend. We were professionally coached by Charles Cochrane, a most impressive personality, who kept us in our place, and certainly stopped us from getting any high ideas about our capabilities. I had to sing a song about a dapper little man called Wally Howarth, a St Thomas's paediatrician. He was always immaculately turned out, with spats and everything - lived at Petworth House and hunted with the Leconfield. My song went like this:

They say that Wally Howarth was in London last weekend
(Chorus) Yes, I don't think
He took a rest from gardening his wardrobe to extend
(Chorus) Yes, I don't think
He called upon the Daily Mail a Sandringham to buy
(Chorus) Yes, I don't think
And when he bought some spats to match the girls all shouted hi
(Chorus) Yes, I don't think
Do you think the little chap was a little bit shy
(Chorus) Yes, I don't think

The show was a considerable success, but I can't help thinking that our amateur approach and the mistakes we made were the main attraction – just as a sponge cake which goes wrong and fails to rise in cooking always seems to taste better than a perfect sponge cake.

I held the Casualty Officer and Anaesthetist job for about a year and a half, and learned a huge amount from doing it. St Thomas's in those days was very much more relaxed and friendly than a big hospital seems to be today. Nowadays there are so many experts specialising in different precise fields that one does not have the contact with patients which one had then – though I must add, of course, that a difficult diagnosis can now be made much more readily. The average medical student and young doctor are fairly basic in their approach to things. We had one chap – called Maxwell – who was always full of ideas outside the field of medicine. He arranged for "the brothel" opposite the hospital to be rebuilt on the lines of a London club, with staff all in green uniforms. This did not last long and St Thomas's House soon went bust. Another thing he used to talk to us about was his concern for the stability of the country just after the war, as huge numbers of men who had been fighting in France poured back to England before civilian industry had been properly organised. Maxwell persuaded many of us to sign on as Special Constables, saying that if things got out of hand there would be a reserve to help the police to keep control.

It is interesting to compare this attitude with attitudes of today. Then, students felt responsible for keeping an eye on the stability of the country – nowadays it seems almost exactly the reverse, with so many students apparently eager to promote unrest, identifying themselves with the forces concerned to upset society. It is strange to think now of students siding with the fuzz! It was some years later, though, before I was required to do anything active as a Special Constable.

It was while I was doing the Casualty Officer's job that a chance incident cropped up that was to change my whole life. A certain Mr. Witherby, a publisher who was a cousin of Harold Allen's, mentioned to me that as it was the end of April he was going to send his horses out to grass with a man called Herbert Stevens at Chain Hill Farm, Wantage: would I like a week's hunting down there first?

I took the train from Paddington to Wantage Road Station (now closed) and there we had to get into the steam tram which took us the remaining 2½ miles into Wantage. How strange and remote I thought as we puffed along the edge of the fields, passing thatched cottages and elm trees. My companions were two stable lads sitting opposite me with saddles on their laps. They told me they had been racing at Kempton Park and were returning to their stables in Letcombe, leaving their horses in a cattle truck at Wantage Road. My remaining fellow-traveller was a silent nun, who was returning to St Mary's Convent.

The puffing tram delivered us to Wantage – the locals

affectionately called the engine Jane Puffer – and we walked up Mill Street to the town square and the Bear Hotel, where a room had been booked for me by Mr. Witherby. This indeed seemed a backwater of Victorian life. There was a very feudal atmosphere in the town then, a relic of the Victorian regime of the first (and last) Lord Wantage, who had great estates around the town. Lord Wantage had been Colonel Lindsay, and had won the V.C. in the Crimean War. He married the daughter (Harriet Loyd) of Lord Overstone, a wealthy banker, who gave her estates at Drayton, Ardington and Lockinge on her marriage. These were the basis of the great Lockinge Estate built up by Colonel Lindsay (later raised to the peerage as Lord Wantage) and his wife.

Lord Wantage approached his responsibilities as a landowner with the same obsessional thoroughness and devotion to high ideals that he had brought to his career as a soldier. He rebuilt villages as model villages, closed the pub in Lockinge and put the landlord in Ardington on a fixed salary, so that he would have no incentive to sell farmworkers more beer than was good for them. He instituted a co-operative shop for his estate workers, so that they could buy goods without contributing to the profits of a monopoly village store. In the agricultural depression of the late Victorian era he bought up farms, not so much to add to his possessions as to help their struggling owners, whom he reinstalled as tenants, and assisted with capital to improve farming techniques.

At its peak the Lockinge Estate was vast – about 60,000 acres. It was said that Lady Wantage could walk from Newbury to Abingdon via Wantage without once stepping off her own land (but, of course, she usually travelled by carriage). Lord and Lady Wantage gave many benefactions to the town of Wantage, and, in return, were regarded as not far short of royalty. This was the background to the almost feudal Wantage to which I was introduced in 1921.

We had a good dinner at the Bear and woke early next morning to find our horses brought to the door by Mr. Witherby's groom boy Carvey. Later he was to become my own groom, a loyal and faithful friend. The meet was at Kingston Bagpuize a few miles from Wantage. It was wonderful to be in the saddle again.

# Chapter 6

# Visiting Australia

The Todds and the Fishers had been great friends in Adelaide from the days of the Observatory. Just before the war in 1913 Guy Fisher had come over to stay with us in Cambridge. He was good company and an excellent tennis player, and he enjoyed the social life of the May balls.

Guy fought with the Australian troops in the Dardanelles. When the war was over and the troops were demobilised, they were offered the choice of a boat straight home from Turkey, or of going back to Australia via England. Guy chose to travel via England, and came to stay with us. He married my sister, Alice, and took her back to Australia with him.

Alice had been asking me to visit them at Pine Hill, Mount Lofty, ever since, but I couldn't think of going out before I qualified. And (as usual) had no money. So when I finished my House Surgeon's job at St Thomas's I set about finding some way of working my passage to Australia.

I went round to shipping office after shipping office P&O, Orient, Commonwealth lines with no success. Then, one Wednesday morning, I went into the office of the Cunard and Australasian Line, and asked a man behind the counter if he wanted a good surgeon. "Why, yes," he said. "But can you sail on Friday?" I said that I could, and he told me to go down to the docks and talk to the captain of the *Port Melbourne*

I reached the docks just before lunch, and duly found the *Port Melbourne*. But the old Irish sea captain said that he could not possibly talk to me before he had had some lunch! I waited, and after lunch we talked business. The *Port Melbourne* was a cargo boat which could carry up to 12 passengers – the maximum number permitted by Board of Trade regulations to travel on a ship without a medical officer. Two rich elderly ladies, apparently exhausted by the London season, had paid £250 apiece for the round trip to Australia and back. When they learned that the ship carried no doctor they said that they would cancel their booking unless a doctor could be got on board: that explained the relief with which my arrival at the shipping office had been greeted.

I was allotted one of the *Port Melbourne's* twelve staterooms for my dispensary and told that I should travel free and be paid one shilling a month. I was also told to turn up in some sort of uniform – a yachting cap and a dark suit were suggested, with a suit of white duck for the Tropics.

On Friday I was on the bridge wearing a yachting cap, and with all my war medals on a presentable dark suit. On that first afternoon I was approached by one of the old ladies, who said "Officer how deep is the ocean here?" I quickly thought of Shakespeare's "Full fathom five", added one for luck, and replied. "About six fathoms, Madam." "Thank you Officer," she said, and went off satisfied. That evening I looked in my diary and found out how many feet there were to a fathom.

Next morning the captain said he wanted to have a word with me about the sick parade. He insisted that my sick parade should take place at 4 o'clock in the afternoon because, he said, it was important that a man should do a day's work before reporting sick – then he would know for certain whether he was sick or not. He was not going to have his crew standing around idly for a morning sick parade.

One afternoon when I was attending to the crew a man

pushed his way to the front of the queue, and demanded instant treatment for a septic finger. I told him to go back and wait his turn, but he became furious and said he was not used to being treated in such a way. I mentioned this to the first officer afterwards, and he said "that was the ship's carpenter who must always be treated with great reverence as he has an unofficial status of petty officer." He warned me that Old Chippy would be sure to find a way of getting his own back.

A few days afterwards he did. We were in fairly rough seas in the Bay of Biscay, and I was lying on my bunk reading. Suddenly, a flood of water came through the ventilator, soaking me, and my bunk. I rushed out on deck to see the retreating figure of the carpenter carrying an empty bucket.

We had a pleasant lot of passengers. One was an old vet who was sailing to New Zealand to start a new life with his family. I was fairly sure that the old boy had T.B., because he was always spitting up blood into all the spitoons on deck. In the evening I used to play chess with the chief engineer, and found it an absorbing mental exercise. The chief engineer won all the way to the Cape, and I won all the games from the Cape to Australia.

I had hoped that we would stop off at all sorts of exciting places on the way out, but was disappointed to learn that the *Port Melbourne* was trying to beat the record time from the Cape to Australia, still held (until our voyage) by a tea clipper from the great days of sail. The captain and crew were a pretty wild lot. I had not been long at sea when I learned the fate of my predecessor on the last occasion that the ship had carried a doctor. He was an elderly man, and when the crew wanted to give him the traditional shave on crossing the equator he ran away. He was chased all round the ship, finally taking refuge by climbing into the rigging. Being elderly he slipped and fell, breaking his neck. He died that same night and was buried at sea.

When we reached the tropics the crew demanded an extra

rum ration. The captain was furious, and asked me to address the crew and tell them that rum was bad for their health. So I had a meeting with the crew, and I duly told them that rum was not the best treatment for heat. They got angry at this, and adopted rather a threatening attitude. The captain then threw his keys to the first mate, telling him to go and get rifles from the arms cupboard for himself and for us. When we had our rifles, we felt a bit braver, and the captain ordered the crew to disperse. One of them shouted, "You're a lot of f..... bastards." This enraged the captain, who ran towards the crew, bursting with fury. As no one would own up to having said anything, he grabbed the nearest man by his hair and gave him such a punch in the belly that he crumpled up on deck. After this the crew dispersed.

That old captain was an odd chap. He was always asking me to tell him about female genitalia – "At what age does a girl feel her helm?" he wanted to know.

At our first Australian port (Williamstown) there was an incident that upset me very much. We had an old Chinaman on board who wanted to enter Australia; to do so, however, he had to pay a tax of £20, and he had only £10. So he asked two of the kitchen stewards to hide him when the port authorities came on board to inspect the ship. The stewards agreed to this, on condition that they were each paid £5. The old man produced the money, and they hid him in the ship's refrigerator. The first I knew of this was being woken up at midnight by two very drunk stewards to see if I could do anything for the Chinaman – they had got drunk on his money, forgotten all about him, and left him in the refrigerator. When they did remember him, he was dead. I refused to give a death certificate. Then (or so it was rumoured) they rowed the body away from the ship, weighted it, and threw it into the sea. I never learned what happened to them, for I left the ship at Melbourne.

I decided to have a look at Sydney before going on to Adelaide, and while in Sydney I was asked by another shipping company to make a trip as ship's doctor to Wellington, New Zealand, and back to Melbourne. One of their ships, without a regular medical officer, had contracted to bring a concert party from New Zealand, and the number of people in the party made it necessary for a doctor to be carried. I was offered £28 a month, and took the job.

On the way back to Australia we had a casualty. One of the passengers was fishing over the side of the ship, and as he cast his line the wind caught it and blew it back, the hook becoming embedded in the eye of another passenger. Like most doctors who are not eye specialists I did not know a great deal about eyes and I was thankful to feel that we were due in Melbourne in two days. Unluckily, a storm blew up, and delayed us for four days. I did what I could for the injured eye, and mercifully it seemed to improve under treatment. As soon as we were able to make port I sent the man to hospital.

Distances in Australia are vast compared with English distances and every journey seemed a great adventure. I loved the countryside with its strange exotic birds and white gum trees and I enjoyed every moment of my travels. It was wonderful to see Alice again – she had had a baby (Bob) since we had last met.

I was introduced to a certain Dr Mercer, a friend of Guy Fisher's, who lived in Adelaide. Dr Mercer was about to be married, and he wanted a locum for two weeks while he went on his honeymoon. He asked me if I would look after his practice while he was away. I liked him, and said that I would. But then there was a snag – I had never driven a car! I told Dr Mercer that if he would show me what to do I was sure that I would have no trouble in driving, and this was settled. Luckily, he had a young gardener who could drive, and it was arranged that he would drive me about for the first day or two, until I got the hang of things. It was an open car, and Dr Mercer had a little white terrier which would dash out of the house whenever the telephone rang and jump on to the folded hood, anticipating a drive into the country. My young gardener-chauffeur liked driving, and unfortunately he liked driving very fast. One day, to my horror, we got home without the little dog, which must have fallen out as we took a corner at speed. There was nothing for it but to go back, to see if we could find him. We did – trotting gallantly along the road about twenty miles away!

When I had nearly finished my two weeks in Adelaide I received a letter from a medical agent to say that a locum was needed urgently for an elderly doctor in the country about 150 miles north of Adelaide, who had gone down with a kidney infection. I agreed to take this job. The practice was in the Maitland peninsula; a wheat-growing area which had recently been reclaimed from desert state by the use of chemical fertilisers. I was struck by the dryness everywhere. We went as far as we could by train and then climbed into a local lorry which was the only means of transport from the railhead, carrying passengers in the back among all the letters, parcels and spares for farm machinery. Most of my calls meant long journeys, the minimum about 25 miles. I would get a message on the local telephone and then I would set out in the doctor's old American car. I was completely on my own, and it is a frightening thought for a doctor to know that he does not have a colleague close at hand from whom to ask a second opinion. I lived at the doctor's bungalow, and was kindly looked after by his wife. Next door to our bungalow was another bungalow which was the local hospital run by an old nurse.

It was with some anxiety that I set off one day on a journey of about 30 miles to answer a frantic telephone call from a mother who said that her baby was having a fit. I eventually arrived amid clouds of dust and went into the homestead, where I found a hysterical mother and a baby having the kind of fit that young children sometimes do get with a high fever. I gave the baby a sedative, and asked the mother for some hot water in which the child could be bathed. She was away some time in getting the water, and I found that she had had to cut up wood, light a fire and warm the water in an old tin in the back yard. When she finally brought the water the strain was suddenly too much and she fell back in a faint. Just at that moment her husband arrived home. He was an epileptic, and the sight of his family in such circumstances immediately brought on an attack. Much to my relief they all eventually recovered and I returned to the doctor's house.

It was only two days after that when a very sick middle-aged farmer was brought to the house in a truck. He said that he had had a sudden violent pain, and had felt sick; when I put a hand on his abdomen it was firm and rigid. I knew that he had a perforated gastric ulcer, and if the hole in his stomach was not mended he would be dead in twelve hours. I collected all the instruments I could find as well as chloroform and ether, and took him into the hospital. The safest of all anaesthetics is open ether, so I mixed 30 parts of ether to one part of chloroform for the anaesthetic and poured this on a piece of cloth as a face mask. As soon as he was unconscious I put the cook in charge, telling her to drop on more of the ether whenever I told her to.

I had assisted in a similar operation at St Thomas's but had never done one by myself. However, with the matron holding the retractors, we sewed up the hole in his stomach, put in a drain and closed the abdomen. A few days later my patient was sitting up in bed, and soon afterwards he was able to go home in his old truck.

The standard rate for a locum in Australia at that time was £10 a week – £3 a week more than the standard rate in England. I was paid £10 a week, and this helped my bank balance. I enjoyed my stay in the Maitland peninsula, and the only major medical difficulty I had was in diagnosing an outbreak of measles among a group of Aborigines. Having been brought up to identify measles from a rash of pink spots, at first I could not make out what the epidemic was – for there were no pink spots However, there were other symptoms that made me think of measles, and as soon as I had identified the disease I was able to treat it successfully.

Off duty I used to play golf with a charming old Anglican parson who said that he loved a game of golf, but never had anyone to play with. The course was sandy and stony, so we left all the sophisticated clubs behind and went round with one iron only.

When I got back to Adelaide I stayed with my sister, Alice. Her Bobby was still very young, and I enjoyed enormous walks around Mount Lofty, with Bobby in a pushchair and my sketch pad tucked in the back. When I was not on nurseman's duty, I enjoyed going down to the Adelaide Club.

Alice had a girl called Eva as a mother's help. She was a most amusing person, adored by the whole family, and she stayed with the family until her death at an advanced age many years later. Eva had been brought up on a homestead in the outback where she lived with her brothers, and she would tell us long stories about her experiences – stories based, no doubt, on an occasional fact, but mostly belonging to a sort of fantasy world of the remembered outback days. One of her favourite tales was of crossing a creek in flood, with her brothers and a flock of sheep. When the leading sheep reached the middle of the creek it stopped, and would go no farther. The whole flock was in danger of being swept away. Eva grasped the situation, grabbed a pair of sheep-shears and bravely battled through the waters to reach the leader. Then she cut away a mass of matted hair which had fallen over its eyes. Once Eva had cut the hair away the sheep was able to see the other side, and led all the other sheep to safety.

The Hawkers were also old friends of my mother's family from the days of the Observatory. Charles Hawker was about my own age; we had known each other at Cambridge, and also had been in hospital together during the war. I was therefore delighted when he suggested that we should go on a two-week trip into the outback, to visit some of the properties that his family owned.

We set off for N. Bungaree in Charles's big American Buick. I was impressed by his mechanical knowledge when he insisted that before we got going we should make sure that a cut-off was fixed to allow the exhaust to go straight out of the engine, without passing through the silencer. It made an appalling noise, but Charles said that it was vital to get the added power from the engine

Bungaree was about 150 miles away, and we considered it a considerable feat to get there in a day. In the 1880s my mother used to go on horseback, taking two long days. A few years back I went out to Australia again to see Charles Hawker, and when I arrived I was told that he had gone the 150 miles to Adelaide for a cocktail party, but would be back shortly. What a difference tarmac roads and the modern motor-car have made. (Whether they have made people any happier is another matter.)

On that first trip of mine to Bungaree the roads were pretty awful, and before we got there our heavy Buick was completely stopped by thick mud. We tried putting on chains, getting ourselves filthy in the process, but we were still stuck. We were almost despairing of ever getting out when Charles's cousin, Walter Hawker, came up in a black 'Tin Lizzie" Ford, which was very high off the ground. Our smart Buick was towed out and we eventually reached North Bungaree.

We stayed four or five days, living with the manager and his wife. At breakfast time I was amazed to see a heap of mashed potato about a foot high, with mutton chops (six to a person) stuck into it so that the dish had the appearance of a pin cushion.

After breakfast we went to the stockyard to get a horse to ride out to see the sheep. It is always a great joke when a Pommy arrives in Australia, and the Australians think it an even greater joke to see him on a horse, as they never expect anyone who is not an Australian to be capable of managing a horse! I kept very quiet about my previous experience, as I knew that if I made any boastful remarks I was sure to be given a buck jumper.

Understatement is a strange characteristic of the Englishman abroad. If a German is invited, say, to play tennis, and asked how good he is, he will say frankly, "I play tennis well; I take part in good contests." And he will turn up for the game in immaculate white trousers and a blazer. But an Englishman asked the same question, even if he is Wimbledon standard, will reply diffidently, "Oh, I do occasionally pat a ball around." And he will turn up in an old pair of trousers and worn out shoes.

I did not like the way the Australian treats his horse – he regards it with little feeling, merely as a means of moving around. I did not do very well at rounding up the sheep and moving them to another pen, so the manager said "if you can't manage, I'll get my dog to do it for you." He gave a few low whistles and the sheep, which I had been struggling with for the best part of an hour, were sent scuttling into the other pen.

The "Jackaroo" is a young farm apprentice, employed on boundary riding, and jobs about the farm. One evening the manager's wife said to our "Jackaroo" that as there was a dance at the township on Saturday night, would it not be a nice idea if he were to take Dr Squires with him? The Jackaroo's face fell a mile - apparently he had a girl friend lined up, and was terrified that I would woo her away from him. So he went into a jealous sulk. Girls were a great rarity in those tough outback places, so he was naturally very anxious. As soon as I understood his anxiety I said that I had a slight cold, and did not feel well enough to go to a dance.

The next station we visited was even more isolated, deep in the outback, and everything was very dry. The manager had pictures of floods in England around his sitting room – to reassure himself that some people could have too much rain! The great treat at this station was a shower fixed up on the verandah of the manager's house, and I was invited to use it. As it was so hot, I welcomed the suggestion. I pulled a curtain round me to hide, as I thought, my naked body from view, but as I was enjoying the water flowing over me I realised that I had carefully hidden myself from the bush, and that the manager's wife was looking at me through the kitchen window. When I apologised for my immodesty, she said "don't worry, it's nice to have a bit of a change up here!"

I don't think I was a great success at that station. If there is one thing I can't bear it is hunting animals from motor cars. The manager here used to go out with the men in an open "Tin Lizzie", standing in the back, and shooting any animals he could see, particularly the Australian wild fox. After half an hour of this I could take no more. I was equally disgusted by the kangaroo hunts. The country teemed with kangaroos, and they did a lot of damage to the young wheat, but all the same it saddened me to see them hunted. The kangaroo learns of an enemy approaching by put its ear to the ground and listening to the vibrations. As we came near with our guns the noble old men of the herd would stand in a row facing us, while the females would run for safety with their "Joeys". When a kangaroo is frightened it forms an excess of saliva and keeps wiping this away with its vestigial front paw. As anxiety mounts, all the fur of its front will be covered in white saliva. A kangaroo by himself will often try and stand in front of a tree and defend himself against hounds by bringing up his huge muscular back leg which can tear a dog apart. Seeing all those gallant old men of the herd defending their women and children was a magnificent sight, and when the manager started firing his rifle at them I am afraid I did not want to go on with the "Sport". Nowadays they hunt kangaroos from Land Rovers, killing about 300 in a night so that all the animal lovers in town can have enough meat for their little dogs.

At the third station Charles wanted me to see sheep shearing in progress. The skill with which the sheep were sheared, and the way in which the animals lay motionless while the shearers were at work, was marvellous to see. The men lived in a wooden shed, where they consumed vast quantities of lamb chops. After each meal they would lie back in their chairs, picking their teeth with penkives, and spitting any bits of meat on to the wooden wall of the shed. They were amused when I remarked that the amount of meat they dug out of their teeth would be equal to an Englishman's meat ration for a year1

Outside the shed all the sheep would be penned to await shearing, except for one which had been selected for tomorrow's chops. This would bleat pitifully in solitary confinement, and I always wanted to let the poor thing out. Life was hard in the outback, and I am sure my feelings were too soft.

On the way home we called on Charles's father, Mickey Hawker, about whom I had heard many stories from my mother. She would refer to him affectionately as "The Old Black Crow". He got this during a dance at Government House, when my mother was still living with her parents at the Observatory. Mickey Hawker was known to be very shy, and all my mother's friends told her that she would never be able to get him to talk. However, my mother was confident that she could get him out of his shell and chatted away to him until eventually he looked at her and said, "We have an old black crow at home." We had tea in his house in the hills, and the only thing I can remember him saying was "If it gets any hotter, I will have to take off my winter combinations."

My sister had just had another baby (Pat) and it was decided that all the family should go over to England for a trip. I had been trying to get a free passage home as ship's doctor, but shipping companies are reluctant to take a doctor if he has relations on board. Guy Fisher, however, had some influence in Adelaide, and he managed to get a passage for me as the ship's doctor on a boat owned by the Commonwealth and Dominion Line called the *Esperance Bay*. We had a peaceful passage from a medical point of view, except for little Pat who developed pneumonia. There were hospital cabins with six beds on board, but these cabins were kept locked when not in use. When Pat became seriously ill, I asked the Captain if I could open them up. We looked everywhere for keys, but could not find them until at last the Captain came across a spare pair. When I did open the door, the Purser and Chief Steward leapt out of bed in a state of undress. It was strictly forbidden for any members of the crew to be found in the passengers' cabins, so that the Purser and the Chief Steward had been bringing their lady friends to my hospital sanctuary. They were furious and insisted that the only reason I wanted to put my sister and niece in the sick bay was to give them better accommodation.

I was careful not to breathe a word to anyone about the incident, as the Captain might have got to hear about it. One must avoid making enemies. It might have seemed better to tell the Captain of the affair, but it would have done no good, and I should have made enemies determined to get their own back.

# Chapter 7

# Start of General Practice in Wantage

"Well, if it isn't Vaughan Squires" said a voice behind me as I stood in the underground between Victoria and Sloane Square. It was George Witherby with whom I had spent a very pleasant week's hunting the previous year. When we came out of the tube at Sloane Square we decided to have a quick pint of beer at the Antelope, a favourite pub of mine off Eaton Square where I used to go in my medical student days.

We exchanged news and he asked me about my plans for the future. I told him that surgery was the branch of medicine which excited me most but that it was difficult to get established. I should have to work up gradually, and it was only when one made a reputation for oneself that one raised one's head above water financially – so it was really a branch for those who had private means. It is exciting, though, because the thrill of medicine is the satisfaction you feel when a patient arrives in dire straits (and may die if nothing is done) and you see him walk out of hospital a fit man again. Often you need only do something simple, such as removing a blockage or letting out a collection of pus, but the thrill of seeing a patient rapidly improve is a joy whatever you have done. I told Witherby about my patient in Australia, and the satisfaction I had felt as he drove out of the hospital in the outback in that old truck – a patient who had been a dying man three weeks previously.

Surgery, then, was my real love in medicine, but I had to accept that it was scarcely practicable for a penniless young doctor just back from Australia to become a surgeon straight away. The alternative was general practice, and there was, indeed, much to be said for it – a pleasant general practice could offer a good life, with, perhaps, the chance of some hunting, and sketching in my spare time. Furthermore there would often be a chance of some surgery in a country practice. Witherby said that he had recently heard from Cyril Birt at Wantage, who wanted a locum, as his partner had become sick. I told him that on that morning I had accepted a post as locum House Physician at the London Chest Hospital, so I would not be free for a month; but that I would certainly telephone Dr Birt. We finished our beer, said goodbye, and hoped we should see each other again (preferably in the saddle!).

When I got back to the London Chest Hospital I telephoned Dr Birt at Wantage. "I want you at once," he said in his usual forceful way. I explained that I had only started that morning at this hospital and I would be there for another month. "No good to me," he said and rang off. That seemed to be that.

A month later, when I had finished my job at the Chest Hospital I made my way over Westminster Bridge to the Dean's office at St Thomas's to see if there were any jobs going; ex-St Thomas's doctors would often telephone or write to the Dean saying that they wanted a house physician, a locum or a partner. In the Dean's office I was given a list of such inquiries, and my eye was caught by the name of Dr Birt of Wantage who needed a locum. I went across the road to St Thomas's House, the students, club, and telephoned Wantage from there. Birt told me that his partner, Jock Kennedy, was still off sick. He had a locum, called Palmer, who had only stayed 3 weeks as he had to take a job elsewhere. "Can you drive a car?" he said. I replied that I could (remembering the last time, and nearly losing Dr Moore's little dog!). "Well, come at once; the job's yours." And so, at the end of the week, on a sunny, crisp day in February, 1923, I caught the 2.15 train from Paddington to Wantage Road. I felt quite nostalgic to see Jane the Puffer (the Wantage steam-tram) at Wantage Road station, gently breathing out steam and smoke. She duly carried me the two miles from Wantage Road station into Wantage Town.

What an attractive place this is, I thought, as I walked by the Bear Hotel, slightly set back from the square with its cobbled courtyard, and remembered the happy week I had spent there the previous year. I made my way to the parish church, and found 2 Priory Road, the address I had been given.

Priory Road formed one side of the churchyard, away from the town square, down a flight of wide steps. What struck me was the lovely old pink brick of the house I had come to. There was a lattice window, at the side, which seemed to date the house to the eighteenth century, but the front had heavy, wooden, ecclesiastical windows. These, I discovered later, had been put in by Street, the Victorian architect, who had restored the parish church, and done much other work on churches and vicarages in the neighbourhood.

I opened the iron gate to the front garden, went up to the door and rang the bell. The door was opened by a neat young maid, dressed in black, with a white apron and cap. I walked into the hall, and was immediately surprised to find how deep the house was stairs to my left with a pleasing mahogany bannister, and a long hall terminating in a glass door, through which I could see the garden.

The maid (Rose Pierpoint) showed me into the drawing room, a large room with fine Georgian proportions. (I later found out that it had been built by Dr Barker, a previous general practitioner, as a billiard room.)

Rose left me, saying that she would make some tea. I wandered across the room to the french windows, which led on to a Victorian cast iron veranda. A huge yew tree, the largest I had ever seen, dominated the garden, growing straight out of the top lawn which swept downhill to a grass tennis court, the orchard and kitchen garden beyond. The top lawn was flanked on the south side by a beautiful old brick wall with a tile cap, which ran down to the greenhouses. On the north side were brick stables, with a pigeon loft in the roof space.

My inspection was interrupted by Rose, who brought both tea and a telephoned message from Dr Birt asking me to go to Theresa Yardley, who lived up the bank in East Hendred, and who had a fever.

I drank my tea quickly and went to the garage with some anxiety to find the old Wolseley which I had been told to use. The garage had been designed to accommodate loose boxes and for pushing in coaches manually, so that a car had to negotiate a double twist backwards to get out. After a few unsuccessful attempts at backing out I finally wedged the car broadside across the exit, and had to go back into the house to ask Rose's advice. She told me to go to George Payne's garage in Newbury Street, where I found a pleasant lad called Tom Spicer, who used to clean Dr Kennedy's car at weekends. He came to help me out and soon got the old Wolseley out of the garage. He kindly accompanied me to East Hendred, explaining on the way how tricky a car it was to drive, because if you went over 40 mph the engine would boil; on the other hand if you drove at less than 40 mph the battery would not charge! Treating Theresa Yardley, who only had a sore throat, was an easy matter after the anxieties of the car!

I was accommodated at 2 Priory Road, which belonged to Dr Kennedy, Dr Birt's partner. He suffered from chest pain, and had been told to take things more easily – it is pleasant to add that he lived to be 87. Dr Kennedy had private means, and he had gone to Allassio on the Mediterranean for a year to convalesce. Since

I was officially Dr Kennedy's locum, as it was he whom I was replacing, it was his job to pay me. The standard rate for a locum then was £1 a day, but Dr Kennedy, being a Scotsman, would pay only £6 10s a week. He argued that since it was a doctor's job to set an example I should no doubt want to go to church on Sunday mornings, which would mean that I should be available only for a half day's work on Sundays! Against this, however, I was looked after very well by Dr Kennedy's staff, getting a good three-course dinner every night, with a tot of whisky afterwards. Dr Kennedy had left special instructions that I should have the whisky, which, he said, was most necessary after a day's work.

I slept in the front room of the house, facing the churchyard. Until I got used to it, I was wakened every night at midnight, three a.m. and six a.m. by the church clock, which not only struck the hour but also, every three hours, played the hymn "O God our help in ages past". Few people telephoned the doctor at night in those days: they would come to the house and ring the Night Bell on the front door. I developed a keen ear for footsteps in the road at night, and could often tell from quick, rather anxious, pattering steps "This one is for me". On one occasion I was woken at 2 a.m. by the bell. I looked out and saw two small boys below the window. "What do you want?" I asked. "My brother Claud has toothache; how much will it cost to take it out?" said one of them. "Five shillings," I said. "My dad only gave us half a crown." So I took him to the hospital and pulled it out for half a crown.

When I went downstairs after my first night I found that Rose had already lit a coal fire in the dining room, and there was a cooked breakfast on the hotplate. I sat at the mahogany table looking through another pair of french windows into the garden, thinking how comfortable and peaceful this all was after London. Little did I realise then that I was to live at 2 Priory Road for the rest of my life.

After that first breakfast I walked up Church Street to the surgery. This was an attractive eighteenth century building facing the church, along the south side of the churchyard. It had originally been used as a cloth merchant's house.

Birt did not believe in spending too much money on the surgery, which was down in the assets of the firm for £300, £200 of which had been mortgaged. There was a central waiting room with flagstones, on to which our consulting rooms opened. Birt showed me the leeches which had arrived from the Radcliffe Infirmary at Oxford that morning. Leeches were still occasionally used at St Thomas's, and Birt said that he used them for mastoids. He would order them from the Radcliffe, and when they were hungry he would put them on a piece of gauze behind the ear where the hot painful swelling of the mastoid was. Soon they would stick their needle-sharp probosces through the skin, suck out the bacteria-laden blood and pus, and bring the swelling down.

I was introduced to the dispenser and bookkeeper, Jock Stewart. He was a very loyal member of the firm, a great character with a strong Scottish accent and a Scottish sense for business. He had a sharp attitude to farmers when they came to pay their bills. "Do we get 10% off for cash?" they would ask. "Aye, that will be all right," he would answer. He would take 10% off when giving them their change, but start the new bill with 10% of the previous one. Jock coped with the dispensing, weighing up all the powders, mixing them with a pestle and mortar and even making the pills on his pill rolling board. He would only dispense for the country patients, the town patients getting their medicine from the chemist in the market square. Dispensing for the country patients was a great help to them. It meant that a man could come to the evening surgery after a day's work – perhaps walking or cycling several miles to do so – and get his medicine on the spot, without his wife having to come in again next day when the chemist was open.

One evening after I had finished the surgery and was about to lock up a man rang the front door bell. He said that he had come to fetch the medicine for his wife, whom I had visited that afternoon in Kingston Lisle – he was sorry he was so late, but he had had to work late. I remembered Jock's saying just before he left that this woman's medicine had not been collected, and that he was going to put it in the post. I thought "If I say to this man 'Don't worry, it is in the post' he will have cycled six miles from Kingston Lisle for nothing. He is worried about his wife; he has come here tired after a day's work on the farm. I can't tell him that it does not matter if her treatment is not started until next morning." So I said instead how glad I was that he had come, because I wanted the treatment to begin that night. I gave him the evening's dose of medicine, and explained that his wife would get the remainder by post in the morning.

I recall that small incident as the first of many that taught me how to be a country doctor. Clinically, it would not have harmed the woman to wait until the morning for her mixture, but medicine is looking after people, and the first need is to try to put yourself in their place. I dare say that making that man feel that he was doing something important to help his wife did as much for both of them as any medicine I could dispense.

The Post Office was a great help to us in our practice. We would wrap up the medicines, sealing them with wax, and leave them at the Wantage sorting office. They would then be delivered free of charge to the patients in the villages.

We also had a surgery boy to run errands for us, and occasionally he would deliver medicines for patients in the town. Among our patients were three old ladies – the Miss Douglases – who lived alone in a big Victorian house in Wantage. Every other week the surgery boy would take round a fortnight's supply of sleeping tablets for them, putting the small parcel through the letter-box. One evening a most distressed Miss Douglas came to the surgery. She had found, she said, the wrappings and the sealing wax from the tablets, but the tablets themselves had been eaten by her small terrier. I told her that the only hope for the dog was not to let it fall asleep, and that I would call first thing in the morning. When I got to the house next morning I found Miss Douglas slumped, fully dressed, on the chaise longue, fast asleep – her first night's sleep without a sedative for goodness knows how long. The dog, however, was wandering aimlessly round the table, trailing its lead – fully awake!

Dr Birt had another assistant in the practice, Dr Campbell Cook. He lived in the town at Beckett House in Wallingford Street, and he had recently installed a new X-Ray machine at his house. At that time the local council was keen to keep the town on gas lighting, to make its new municipal gasworks pay, so there was little electricity available. To work the X-Ray machine a special cable had to be run from a local foundry to Beckett House. The machine was undoubtedly useful and when Cook left the practice I brought it to 2 Priory Road and put it in the disused stables. The site, however, was rather too damp for it, and often when one turned it on there would be huge flashes and sparks. I managed to improve things somewhat by installing an electric fire.

We would see a variety of patients at our morning surgery sessions – some from the town, and some who had come in from the surrounding villages. The fee for a consultation was five shillings unless they belonged to the Benevolent Club when it would be three shillings and sixpence. This covered the cost of the consultation, and two days of medicine.

After morning surgery we would visit patients in the cottage hospital at Belmont. This was run by a wonderful old woman called Matron Pike. Not only did she run the hospital in the day, but if we were anxious about a particular patient would often sit up with him all night. She was paid £60 a year and she was in charge of six probationers, whom she trained in nursing in return for their work. The probationers got £25 a year, and their uniform.

Matron Pike liked her discipline. One morning I went to see a young lad who was about due to be discharged. I intended to tell him that he could go home. Before I could do so, however, the Matron asked if she could have a word with me. She explained that the lad, who was obviously well again, had been larking about and disturbing the other patients, so she slapped his bottom, hard. There was still a red mark on his buttocks – could he be kept in until it went away? I duly told the boy's mother that her son seemed to have developed a slight cold, and I thought it would be wiser if he stayed in hospital till the weekend.

At the time of my arrival in Wantage Dr Birt was trying to persuade the hospital's management committee to install a lift. The committee, however, decided that as there was now a healthy young locum (me) to carry post-operative patients up the stairs, a lift was an unnecessary expense.

I looked forward to my country rounds in Dr Kennedy's old Wolseley in the afternoons. The countryside around Wantage is glorious. It lies at the foot of the great chalk Downs from whose summit at White Horse Hill you can see (or so it is said for I have never counted them) no fewer than thirty counties! In the Vale – the Vale of the White Horse – and on the springline of the Downs there are enchanting villages – Childrey, the Letcombes (Regis and Bassett), the Hendreds (East and West) the Hanneys (East and West), Goosey, with its enormous village green, Uffington, where Thomas Hughes of *Tom Brown's Schooldays* had his village schooling before going on to Rugby, and a covey of other small, secluded places. Within the space of a few miles there are two completely different types of countryside – the rounded, turf-covered chalk of the Downs, and the lush, well-watered Vale, criss-crossed by streams and streamlets that carry away the water percolating through the chalk.

Building materials in the villages and hamlets are as varied as the countryside. Northwards towards Faringdon you are entering Cotswold country, and begin to meet the lovely, honey-coloured Cotswold stone. The clay of the Vale of the White Horse provides brick, often used with a local ragstone in a mixture of stone and brick, and, in the very old houses, with timber framing and a wattle-and-daub infill. On the foothills of the Downs you find the chalk itself used as building material, cut into blocks so thick and hard that they can last for centuries. There are some fine examples of chalk building at Uffington and Compton Beauchamp. Yet another fascinating building material comes from those mysterious stones called sarsens, not native to the Downs but brought by glaciers during the distant Ice Ages. Lambourn has a particularly exciting array of sarsens in houses, and around the churchyard.

The chalk soil of the Downs is porous, so that water runs straight through, to emerge in springs when it meets a bed of clay or some non-porous rock. This leaves the surface of the Downs remarkably dry even after heavy rain, and the springy turf that covers the chalk is ideal for horses, creating those marvellous gallops that have long been used by trainers. It was – and is still – a fine sight to come across a string of perhaps thirty thoroughbreds making their way towards the Downs for exercise.

Before the First World War a doctor's country visits would almost all be made on horseback, but by my time the horse was rapidly being replaced by the motor car. One of my predecessors at 2 Priory Road, Dr Barker, always made his rounds on a small chestnut cob, accompanied by an old dog, which would stay outside and hold the horse while the doctor called on a patient. Dr Barker suffered badly from gout. One day he was asked to visit East Hendred to vaccinate the infant son of the innkeeper at The Plough. He went as a matter of course, but when he got there his gout was so bad that he rapped on the window of the inn and asked if the child could be handed out to him to save him having to dismount. This was duly done, and the little boy was vaccinated lying across the saddle of Dr Barker's horse.

Horses were still useful in my time, but we used them only when we had to visit a particularly isolated farm; we had to go through floods to villages in the Vale – the River Ock and its many tributaries are liable to severe flooding after heavy rain, or the melting of a heavy snowfall. We had a regular drill for such occasions: Dr Birt would send his groom ahead, to the limit of the hard road leading to some downland farm, to the edge of the flood water in the Vale, and one of us would then go by car to meet the horse, and continue our journey by horseback. The roads to Charney Bassett and the Hanneys were particularly subject to flooding, and I had often to ride through two or three feet of water to visit patients in those villages.

On one occasion Dr Birt asked me to ride with him across the Downs to see a patient at Lattin Down. This meant taking a short cut across two farms, called Furzevick and Pewit farms. As we passed close to Pewit Farm an old woman ran out and shouted to us to go back. Birt said that we were doctors riding to visit a patient, and that he had no intention of going a long way round by road. "I'll soon see about that," said the old woman. She ran back to the house, got her husband's shotgun, and let it off close to the horses' heads. They reared up, but we were able to control them and galloped off.

Shortly before I joined the practice Dr Birt had been called to a lonely farm beyond the Ridgeway, to attend a woman who was said to be bleeding from a threatened miscarriage, and whose husband was mentally disturbed. He rode out to the farm, and tied his horse outside the door. When he went in he found the farmer's wife cowering in one corner, and the farmer came at him with a carving knife, shouting "Leave my wife alone." Birt picked up the kitchen table by its legs, and, using it as a shield, charged the man, telling the wife to run for the horse. Leaving the husband pinned in a corner by the table-top he, too, then ran for the horse, and with the woman on the saddle in front of him rode as hard as he could to Belmont hospital. By the time they got there the miscarriage was complete, but the woman was safe, and made a good recovery.

We used to see many cases of lobar pneumonia, for which in those days we had neither sulphonamides nor antibiotics – we had only expectorants for the cough, and Dover's Powders to relieve the pain. These pneumonias, which nowadays have virtually disappeared, used to be sadly common, especially among young people. The patient would run a high fever for some days, often reaching a temperature of 105º and have great difficulty in breathing. Often, too, he or she would be delirious. The sound from the infected lung when the patient said "Ninety-nine" was unmistakeable – it was as if he had a clothes' peg on his nose. On the sixth to seventh day one would know how the disease was going to progress; either the patient would start bringing up copious blood-stained sputum, or else he would die. This was known as "the crisis", and the relatives would sit up all night to wait hopefully to see which way things would go. Before the development of antibiotics people had only their bodies' own immunities to fight bacteria – pneumonia was literally a fight for life. Sometimes a patient would form pus in the lungs. We would then get him to hospital and draw off the pus with a needle.

I used to have a gay social life, as a spare male was always useful to make up numbers at dinner and tennis parties. There were tennis parties on grass courts every weekend in the summer, and it was a peaceful way of spending the afternoon – if one was not actually playing one would be sitting outside the court chatting to the other members of the party.

Dr Birt liked to go hunting three days a week, which somewhat irritated the other partners. Soon after I came to Wantage I saved up enough to have my first day's hunting. The meet was at Denchworth and I hired a horse for £3 from a man at Faringdon who kept stables: this, together with the cap collection of £2 at the meet, meant that it was going to cost £5 for the day. Everything started well, but early in the afternoon my horse joined about five others, and we ran abreast at Rosy Brook hoping to clear it. The other four just managed to scramble out by dropping their hind legs, but my horse mistimed it, and landed right in the middle of the brook. I waded to the far bank, while he went upstream to emerge where the brook shallowed and the bank was lower. To my horror, he had no bridle! Seeing the likelihood of my £5 day's hunting cantering away, I flung my arms round his neck. At that moment old Maurice Reade, from Baulking Green, rode by, and he shouted down to me "What's the matter, doc? With all the pretty girls who want kissing in the neighbourhood, why do you have to choose your horse? Come back to Baulking Green and I will lend you another bridle." I went back to the Reades at Baulking Green next day for Sunday tea, but we had no success in finding the bridle in the brook. So I had to pay the stables an extra thirty shillings for the loss.

It seems incredible to think that when I started in general practice at Wantage there was no obstetrician at the Radcliffe Infirmary in Oxford, so we had no one from whom we could get a second opinion in maternity cases. We just had to get on with things as best as we could. I used to enjoy the maternity work, and we did a fair amount: there is something peculiarly satisfying in spending some hours with a patient, helping with all her difficulties, and then suddenly it is all over, and a baby is born.

A patient then might decide to do without a doctor, and book a midwife for her confinement for thirty shillings. The doctor cost £2. With a normal confinement the midwife could cope well enough on her own, but there could be real trouble if something went wrong, and either the patient or the midwife was reluctant to call a doctor in good time. In such cases one might arrive to find a patient with an obstructed labour in dire straits. How much better things are now, when doctor and midwife work side by side in close cooperation.

If a doctor was booked for a confinement in the 1920s, he was expected to earn his £2 by seeing the whole thing through. This called for nice judgement in timing, to avoid having to hang about for hours waiting for a birth. Unless one was exceptionally lucky, there was usually an hour or two of waiting for that little head to appear. I recall those confinements vividly, in rooms covered carefully with newspapers, arranged in a tidy patchwork on the bed and floor. I tried to avoid boredom by reading those old newspapers, and sometimes – I am ashamed to say - I have recommended that it would be a wise precaution to bring a few more newspapers into the room. I did not do any Caesarian sections, but Dr Campbell Cook used occasionally to do them in the Belmont hospital.

A woman bleeding before she produces her baby creates a very worrying situation for an obstetrician, because if the uterus is empty it will contract and stop the bleeding, but if the infant is still inside this can't be done and a critical condition may arise. This can happen if the afterbirth has grown to block the exit of the uterus so that the baby is squeezed out, with its head forced through a mass of tissue disrupting all the blood vessels. In such a situation, the mother can lose a vast amount of blood very quickly from which she may not recover.

Nowadays this is usually recognised before labour has started, and a Caesarian section is performed in the security of a hospital. But when one was faced with such an emergency in an isolated farm the situation was very difficult. Sometimes I would have to push the baby back into the uterus, turn it, grab hold of a leg and pull it down, and then hang a pound weight on the end of the baby's foot with a bandage. This would act as a stopper and counter the worst bleeding. I would then have some anxious minutes in which to deliver the baby as quickly as possible as a breech birth before too much blood was lost.

One particular maternity case stands out in my memory. I had a call to Blackacres Farm one evening to a woman who had come to stay from London, and who was due to have a baby. By the time I arrived the baby was well on the way, and I duly delivered it. I went back a day or two later to see how mother and baby were getting on, and I found that the mother had developed a fever, which caused me some anxiety. Within a few days she was panting for breath, with a relentless cough and pain in the chest – and I knew that she had pneumonia. I had my usual sense of helplessness – there was so little that one could do for pneumonia in those days. Occasionally one might, perhaps, give a little morphia, but any really powerful drug to relieve pain and to provide a little rest from that terrible cough might equally depress respiration and cause the patient to stop breathing for ever. My patient clung on to life, and for about six weeks I drove the six miles to see her every other day. I could at least try to encourage her morale – nothing is more tragic than for a mother to die in childbirth, and a time which should bring joy turns into grief. I did my best to appear confident and cheerful, and I used to greet the baby by saying "Hullo, Mr. Whiskers". That mother nearly died many times, but I'm thankful to say that eventually she did recover. The sequel came 25 years later. The family had moved away but one day, shortly after I had come home from the Second World War, a patient called to see me in the same Church Street surgery from which I had been summoned to attend that mother. He said "You don't remember me, and I don't remember you, but I am Whiskers." That is the sort of continuity which makes general practice so rewarding, and so worthwhile.

I went on living by myself in Dr Kennedy's house, enjoying my social life, as well as the fascinating contact one had with patients and their families, helping to sort out many of their problems.

Just before Christmas 1923 I received a letter from Dr Kennedy insisting that I should go down to his cellar and select for myself a bottle of his favourite vintage port. I mentioned this to the cook, who said that she would fetch it from the cellar, but I implored her not to. That evening, however, the bottle was produced for me, poured out into a decanter without leaving the sediment, and without straining – it so that it was as murky as pond water, and quite undrinkable. I did not like to mention this to the cook for fear of hurting her feelings, so I had to write to Dr Kennedy in Italy thanking him for the bottle, saying how delicious it had been. In the New Year the whisky supply ran out. As I had been having only one small tot each night, I was rather mystified, but as whisky then was only 7/6 a bottle I ordered a fresh supply from the Wantage stores.

That spring Dr Kennedy and his family came home from Italy. The evening of their return produced a most embarrassing situation. Mrs. Kennedy enjoyed a bottle of good claret, and the cook was asked to get one from the cellar. She sent the maid back with a message that the cellar was empty! I then added that the whisky had run out some months previously, and that I had been buying my own. As for the wine, I explained that I had had only the one bottle of port that Dr Kennedy had invited me to have at Christmas. I began to understand why the cook had been so anxious for me not to go down into the cellars! Questioning of the maids revealed that the cook would get drunk in her bedroom every night, getting through a bottle a night. This was a sad business, but at least my name was cleared.

Here I shall depart briefly from the strict chronology of events to relate my own progress in the practice over the next few years. Later in the year of his return to England, Dr Kennedy decided to retire. That left Dr Birt as the sole remaining partner in the practice, Dr Campbell Cook, who was still working as an assistant, and me. I liked Campbell Cook; he had his FRCS, and we used to do a lot of surgery together. He was a very conscientious doctor, and a much gentler man than Birt. But Birt, in spite of his rather arrogant manner, was well-liked. Trouble came over Birt's hunting. Campbell Cook considered it outrageous that Birt should go off hunting three days a week, and there was a great row, after which Campbell Cook decided to leave. It was a foolish decision, because if only he had realised what opportunities there were in the practice, and if only he had waited, he would soon have become a partner. But he did not wait, and departed.

So at the end of 1924 the only remaining doctors in the practice were Dr Birt and myself, officially still only Dr Kennedy's locum. I was very disappointed when Birt told me one evening that he had decided to take in as a partner a certain Dr Palmer, who had worked as a locum for only two weeks about a couple of years before. I was invited to stay on as an assistant at £800 a year.

I did not mention to Dr Birt what I felt at not being offered even a very junior partnership. I wanted to stay in the practice, so I said that I would accept a job as assistant, but that I felt he ought to pay me £1,000 a year – the salary that had been paid to Dr Campbell Cook. After some discussion I settled for £900, plus 10% of the profits from the practice over £6,000 a year, which would add an extra £50 or so to my pay.

Dr Palmer took over the house at 2 Priory Road, and I became a paying guest there. The house had not belonged to Dr Kennedy, but to the Lockinge Estate – the rent was £84 a year. The Lockinge Estate also had the house wired for electricity (at a cost of £45) to provide power for the X-ray machine I had acquired from Dr Campbell Cooke. Dr Palmer's Aunt Jenny came to Wantage to look after us, and I became very fond of her.

With Dr Kennedy went the old Wolseley, so I made a trip to Oxford to see what I could buy. I eventually settled for a Morris Cowley, which cost £134 – new. As an ex-Serviceman I was given a year's free insurance for the car by the (then) Sir William Morris. With my new-found wealth (rather more than double what I had been getting as a locum) I also acquired a lovely old

*Back of the old surgery in Church Street. Self, Dr Birt and Willie Dawson*

grandfather clock. I had long wanted a grandfather clock, and had been keeping my eyes open for any that might be for sale, and suddenly a real beauty was offered near Abingdon. The owner wanted £20 for it, but I felt that I couldn't afford £20, so I offered £10. This was rejected, and there the matter rested until the owner suddenly fell ill and I was called to attend him as a patient. He was obviously pleased with my treatment, for he said that I could have the clock for £12, provided that I took it away. I was able to lay it across my Morris Cowley by lowering the windscreen (you could raise and lower windscreens in those days) and I took it proudly back to Priory Road. I was noticed driving through Wantage and a rumour quickly went round the town that the young doctor had taken to making his own coffins!

My life in the practice continued happily enough, but things did not go smoothly between the partners. It was the old story – Dr Palmer felt that he was getting an unfair share of the work because of Dr Birt's insistence on hunting three days a week. One day in 1926 Dr Palmer said that he wanted to talk to me. He then told me that he was fed up with Birt's hunting, and felt that we ought to try to get him out of the practice: if this could be done, would I come in as a partner? I replied that this was a matter between Dr Palmer and Dr Birt, and that Palmer must talk to Birt without involving me. A couple of days later Dr Birt came to see me. He said he felt that Palmer was not happy in the practice: if he could get rid of Palmer, would I become a partner? I made the same reply as I had made to Palmer: the question of whether one or other of the existing partners should leave the practice was a private matter between them, and really should not be discussed with me, who was only an assistant working for the practice.

Eventually, Palmer decided to go, and took up a resident's post in a mental hospital. Birt then formally offered me a partnership, at a cost of £6,000 for a one-third share of the goodwill of the practice. Buying a practice, or a partnership in a practice, was the normal thing in those days: a practice was a business, and the goodwill belonged to whoever had founded it, or bought it. Selling a practice, or a share in a practice, was a means of providing for retirement, and there were specialist agencies to help young doctors with the finance of entering a practice, in much the same way as a building society helps with buying a house. I was happy to accept Dr Birt's offer. For all his hunting and occasionally arrogant manner, he was a sound doctor, and he was well-respected by the patients. So the firm became Birt and Squires, and once again I was on my own at 2 Priory Road. I took on the tenancy myself, and my parents came to help me settle into what was now my own house. They suggested that I should invite Mr. and Mrs. Leach from Cambridge to come and work for me, Mr. Leach as my butler, Mrs. Leach as cook. They accepted, and the arrangement worked very well. We had taken on another young assistant, Dr Dawson so that there were two bachelors to be looked after.

# Chapter 8

# Responsibilities

1926 was a crowded year. Shortly before the troubles in the practice came to a head (as related in the last chapter) I had a letter from St Thomas's Hospital reminding me that I had signed on as a Special Constable, and warning me that I might be required to serve with the Constabulary to deal with the wave of strikes, marches and other forms of industrial unrest then sweeping the country. The same week brought a second letter, ordering me to report to St Thomas's, to take charge of a unit of twelve men, some, like myself, old St Thomas's men, some still medical students. As soon as I got to the hospital I was instructed to march my unit through Lambeth to the Elephant and Castle, and report to the police station there.

We were met by an enormous police sergeant, who told us that our job was to clear the Old Kent Road, where crowds of strikers and marchers were disrupting traffic. He gave us a truncheon apiece and said, "Go like hell and charge – they'll soon run. Don't hit anybody on the head because that may knock a man out, and then you'll have all the difficulty of dealing with an unconscious body. If you have to hit anybody, hit on the shoulder – that hurts the collar-bone and stops a man hitting back at you."

When we saw the seething mass of people in the Old Kent Road we thought that we had been given an impossible task, and I also thought privately that the huge old police sergeant would scarcely be able to manoeuvre his bulk to tackle anybody. But he tucked his overcoat into his belt in a most businesslike fashion and shouted "Charge!" As we went into action the crowd scattered in all directions. From upstairs windows people hurled garbage and emptied slop pails over us, but after about an hour the road was clear. An old hansom cab came round the corner, the horse trotting delicately down the empty road. It looked for a moment as if we had cleared the road especially for him.

We spent a week at the Borough Police Station at the Elephant and Castle, going out on point duty, or escorting food vans. I was doing what I supposed to be my duty, but the whole affair distressed me very much. As a doctor, I had the privilege of treating men and women of all classes as equals: now, for the first time, I had the feeling that I was involved in a class war, with the middle classes who had possessions fighting against the working classes who had not. The strikers were not asking for huge wages they were fighting for food for their families. But the life of the nation had to go on, and the bread vans had to get through. Half a dozen of us would hide in a van, and when the strikers stopped it and tried to get at the bread they would find it guarded.

A horrible incident occurred one day when I was on point duty. A little Cockney came up to me and said, "Hullo, Guv'nor. Sorry to see you here. When I last saw you ten years ago we were fighting on the same side." I recognised him as one of the troopers who had been in my division on the Western Front.

I was thankful to get back to Wantage. Even in peaceful Wantage, however, there was poverty: not, perhaps, so glaring as in London and the big industrial towns, but much more visible than poverty is now. You seldom see tramps nowadays – in the twenties they were a familiar sight, making their way from workhouse to workhouse, most of them desperately trying to find a job. They would knock on doors, offering to look after horses, dig the garden, anything, and offering to accept less than whatever one might be paying already. The old Poor Law in force then made some provision for the relief of poverty, but it was often harsh and hateful in its working. As medical officers we had to keep a register of impoverished families in the neighbourhood, and send this every week to the Poor Law Officer, who was responsible to the Guardians of the Poor appointed to administer parish relief. The Guardians would consider each case, and decide whether to give relief in money, or to hand out tickets, which could be used in local shops, for bread, meat and vegetables. This was one of the things that people hated – you could not use a bread ticket without telling the shopkeeper and all your neighbours that you were on parish relief.

The Guardians were also responsible for the Workhouse, a large rambling building up the Manor Road. This was run by a warden and his wife, and had 47 beds. At the entrance there was a grim sign with two arrows, one directing people to the office, the other to the mortuary. About half the beds in the Workhouse were occupied by permanent residents, the others kept for "travellers" (tramps). Workhouses in England were supposed to be roughly a day's walking distance apart: our tramps had usually walked from Wallingford, and they would spend a day or two in Wantage before walking on to the next workhouse at Hungerford.

Although the word "workhouse" is associated with harsh treatment of the poor, the place itself was often useful – an elderly person unable to look after himself could almost always get a bed there. There were separate male and female wards, and the tradition – quite needless – of strict segregation of the sexes often caused deep distress: an elderly couple, who, perhaps, had lived together all their lives, would be separated if they had to go to the Workhouse. I used to feel that there would have been no real difficulty in providing a few one-room flats where old couples could have shared their last days.

I had a lot to do with the Workhouse, for Dr Birt was officially the Medical Officer, and as he was so often away hunting I normally did most of the work. One day a great scandal occurred. There was an elderly man, universally known as Boy Charlie, who had spent most of his life in the Workhouse, and who paid for his keep by doing odd jobs about the place. One day the Warden's wife found him in the Women's Section, actually kissing one of the inmates! An emergency meeting of the Workhouse Committee was called at once; among the members were Lord Goschen from Ardington House, Tommy Loyd from Lockinge House, and me, representing the Medical Officer. The whole thing was conducted like a court martial. First Boy Charlie was brought in and interrogated, and then the frightened little old lady. She had a pathetically whiskery face, and was quite the plainest person I had ever seen. After the offenders had been taken away, the committee was left to consider its judgement. I felt I couldn't stand the solemnity any more, so I stood up and said, "Boy Charlie has worked here all his life, running errands and making himself useful with all sorts of little jobs. Maybe he has strayed from the paths of virtue, but after seeing both the participants my own feeling is that he should be given a medal rather than a reprimand. "Tommy Loyd at once came down on my side. He burst out laughing and said "I agree with Dr Squires." That swung the issue, and the case was dismissed.

In addition to his post as Medical Officer of Health, Dr Birt was also Public Vaccinator. Vaccination then was compulsory, as it remained until after the Second World War, and most children (unless there was some medical reason against it) were vaccinated in infancy. There was an escape clause for people who were conscientiously opposed to vaccination – they could make a declaration before a magistrate, and obtain exemption for their children. But most people accepted vaccination as a good thing, and all vaccinations carried out by a Public Vaccinator were free to the patient. We were paid five shillings for each vaccination by the Government.

I never saw an actual case of smallpox in Wantage, but smallpox scares were not infrequent. In the early stages of the disease it is often difficult to distinguish between smallpox and a case of severe chickenpox. On several occasions we opened up the small isolation hospital which Lord Wantage had built in his woods near the Downs, only to close it again when we realised that we were dealing with no more than chickenpox. During smallpox scares I had to go to the Workhouse every evening to carry out an examination of all the inmates, who would be drawn up ready for me, standing naked at the end of their beds. This was by no means an unnecessary routine, for with the constant influx of tramps there was a real possibility that someone from an infected area might introduce the disease. There is precisely the same problem still with air travel from some place where there is a smallpox epidemic, only nowadays the examination is carried

*Self enjoying a drink with cousin Willie Bragg and wife Alice*

out at international airports. We were particularly concerned with tramps who had come from anywhere round Gloucester. There was a doctor in Gloucester then who ran a campaign against vaccination, with the results that there were more unvaccinated people around Gloucester, with a higher risk of smallpox, than in most other parts of the country.

When I came to Wantage the only hospital was the small one at Belmont, about which I have already written. A bigger and better-equipped hospital was needed to serve the town and the surrounding villages, and years of effort went into the task of raising the £12,000 which, it was estimated, such a hospital would cost. We had dances, carnivals, jumble sales and all sorts of activities to raise funds for the hospital, and I used to go round the villages to talk at fund-raising meetings. All the doctors in the area subscribed, and a bed could be endowed in the name of a donor for £50. In spite of the hard times, people were generous in giving money towards the hospital, and at last we could go ahead and build. There was a hitch at the last moment, because when the date came for closing the old hospital the new one was not quite ready. We had been running down the old hospital and most of the remaining patients could go home, but I had one patient with pneumonia who was too ill to be sent home. I had quite a row with Dr Birt about him. Birt said "Send him to the Workhouse, old chap. He'll be all right." I said that I could not possibly send a man as ill as he was into the crowded male ward at the Workhouse, and I insisted that he should stay where he was. So he did, and the old hospital stayed open about ten days longer than had been planned. My patient was very ill indeed. He developed pus in the chest cavity, which I managed to relieve with a drainage tube. I am happy to say that he got over the pneumonia in the end.

Even then the new hospital was not quite out of trouble. We had raised £12,000 for it, but the final cost came to £15,000, so fund-raising had to continue. It is astonishing to think now what could be built for £15,000 only fifty years ago.

# Chapter 9

# Private Life

The Good Life for a man (or so I was told in youth) requires three things – a dog, a horse and a woman, and in that order! My patients were always telling me that it was time I thought of getting married, but I used to reply guardedly that I wasn't going to let my heart rule my head, and that as I had yet to acquire a dog and a horse of my own, marriage could be considered in due course.

Dr Kennedy had had a fine Alsatian called Juno who became very attached to me. When the Kennedys were moving from 2 Priory Road I went to stay temporarily at the Bear Hotel, and to get Juno out of the way I took her with me. The hotel staff did not altogether approve: Juno would never leave my side, and when I went to the Gents, she would sit outside the door and allow no one else to go in until I came out.

When the Kennedys finally left Wantage, of course Juno had to go with them, so I bought an Alsatian pup, which I called Judy. Soon after she arrived she developed eczema, but I managed to nurse her through it, and she grew into a very fine bitch. Like most Alsatians she was devoted to one person, and she became very fond of me, and I of her. She used to come with me when I went riding on the Downs, though she rather liked to jump over sheep-fences, and sometimes I had to go after her with a riding whip. Sheep are a temptation to any dog, but it is a temptation that must be resisted sternly. Judy always came with me in the Morris Cowley when I went on my rounds. One of the jobs which Dr Birt had handed over to me was that of Medical Officer to the nuns at St Mary's Convent in Wantage. One afternoon when I was visiting a nun and had left Judy in the car outside the convent, the door suddenly burst open and Judy jumped on the terrified nun's bed.

In 1921 my Uncle Will (Sir William) Bragg and Aunt Gwen came to stay with me. Uncle Will had been President of the British Society for the Advancement of Science and he was due to hand over his honorary office to his successor, the Prince of Wales (later Edward VIII) at a ceremony at Magdalen College, Oxford. This was to take place at a garden party at the college, and I was invited. Uncle Will and Aunt Gwen had gone to Oxford the day before to spend the night there, and I drove over in my Morris Cowley, Judy automatically coming with me. When I got to the Magdalen gateway I was told that dogs were not allowed in, so I left Judy tied to the steering wheel of the car. I joined other guests at the garden party and was enjoying myself when suddenly there

*My mother, known as the March her sister and her husband, Sir William Bragg at Priory Road*

was an urgent announcement over a loudspeaker: would the owner of an Alsatian dog go at once to the college gate?

I rushed off, to find a bunch of anxious-looking people collected at the gate, with Judy standing between them and the Prince of Wales, making it plain by her growls that she was not disposed to allow the Prince to enter. I pacified Judy, and the Royal Visit was able to proceed. Everyone appeared exceedingly embarrassed except the Prince of Wales, who, perhaps, was privately relieved to get out of a few minutes of speechmaking.

For all his eminence as a scientist, Uncle Will was a gentle, kindly person. The death in the war of their son and my close friend Bob Bragg had been a tragic blow, and perhaps because Bob and I, almost of an age, had been so close to one another, they treated me almost as a son: their house in London was a second home to me. When they stayed with me at Wantage we went for a long walk over the Downs, along the Ridgeway. Uncle Will could talk about the latest developments in physics in such simple, unassuming terms that he made one feel that one was not as stupid as one thought – a marvellous gift from a brilliant brain to ordinary mortals. I recall him saying to me once that the one job in the world he really coveted was the Cavendish Chair of Physics at Cambridge. "Rutherford is there," he added, "at work on splitting the atom. I pray that he will never succeed."

There is a charming true story about Uncle Will after he had been attending some meeting at the Royal Institution in London. He felt that he would like a quiet walk in Hyde Park. The daffodils were just out, and he sat on a park bench to look at them. While he was sitting there a park attendant came by with a broom, sweeping the edges of the grass. He said "Good day" to Uncle Will, and they got into conversation, the park attendant saying how much pleasure he got from the lawns and trees and flowers, and how much satisfaction it gave him to be able to help to keep the park tidy. "The trouble, Sir," he concluded, is that there are too many scientists in the world. They are the cause of all our worries." Uncle Will did not disclose who he was.

Having acquired a good dog, the next thing was to find a good horse. Dr Birt had always had good horses. When Lady Wantage died she left him £500, which thrilled him very much. A day or so after he had received the money he was driving down from London, and came up behind a horse with a most beautiful action. He put his car in bottom gear and followed slowly behind the horse until the rider turned into a stable. He went in after him, and bought the horse. It gave him a most beautiful ride home, but in the hunting field, unhappily, it used to tire easily, and a day's hunting left it so exhausted that it would not eat.

When I was staying at the Bear Hotel while the Kennedys moved house I had met some people called Thorburn, a most charming couple who had got so fed up with the responsibilities of running a house that they moved into the hotel permanently. They brought their horses with them, and kept them in the hotel stables. The Thorburns remained my friends for many years, and I bought my first horse from Mr. Thorburn for £40. She was a mare called Dynamite, and was – or rather had been – a fine animal. She was still a good ride, but used to blow a bit if you wanted any great speed out of her. She was as keen as mustard, however, and gave me some wonderful days hunting. She loved to keep well up in front, and when she really got going she would take hold of things on her own. The only way I could control her was to ride her on a twisted nose-band, which would tighten on pulling the reins.

Cyril Kent, a member of an old Wantage family who kept a big ironmonger's shop and had property all over the town, used to keep his own horses in stables next door to the shop, and behind the King Alfred's Head public house. The licensee was a man called Marriot who had worked in racing stables. He helped to look after Mr Kent's horses, and when I bought Dynamite he said that he would look after her as well. This did not turn out a satisfactory arangement. Marriot had been brought up to keep horses in condition by frequent riding-out, and he felt that he must look after Dynamite in the same way. It used to madden me when I had an hour or so to spare for a ride between patients to go to the stables only to find that Dynamite was out with Marriot.

I made a mistake in entering her for the Farmers' and Subscribers' Race in the Old Berkshire Point-to-Point at Faringdon. She nearly came down at the first fence, but she was so game that she kept going. Three fences before the end a horse on my right refused, which spoiled Dynamite's timing, and she caught her hind legs on the top. Next came the spread of the water jump, and she just didn't have the speed to clear the brook on the far side. However, we scrambled out to face the last jump, and gallant Dynamite just could not do it. For the first time in her life she refused. The locals in the crowd all shouted at me, "Come on, Doc. Over that fence, and there's a fiver for you!" But it was no good; poor Dynamite was too exhausted to jump.

That race seemed to take a lot of heart out of her, and soon afterwards I gave her to a farmer who said that he would try to breed from her. She did have a foal, but it got jaundice and died soon after birth. After this brave act of motherhood Dynamite deteriorated, and had to be put down by the vet. I insisted that this must be done in a field where she was used to living. Nothing is more horrible than the frenzy horses get into when they are penned outside a slaughterhouse and can smell the blood of their fellows who have been slaughtered. I have always insisted that when any animal of mine has had to be put down, it is done in a field.

I bought my second horse in a rather odd way. He was a curious animal, with a mind so much his own that if he decided to go a certain way he would go that way, whatever his rider tried to do. He also had a strange habit of putting down his forefeet and suddenly turning at right angles when cantering along. He had belonged to Bob Pike, of Manor Farm, Lyford. One market day Bob offered to give the horse to a butcher, who was a friend of his, if he could ride him from Lyford to the Bear Hotel, have a pint of beer, and ride him back. For some reason the horse was in a good mood that day, for he trotted into Wantage readily enough, and quietly trotted back again to Lyford. So the butcher won the horse.

I first met him at the Point-to-Point in which I was riding Dynamite. The butcher was riding him, and leading the field, but at the first jump the horse did one of his right-angle turns, and threw the butcher. He went on to gallop riderless round the course. Since poor old Dynamite was not much good after that race, I approached the butcher and asked if I could buy his horse. We settled on a price of £10. Not long afterwards I heard the butcher saying in a pub, "What a fool that doctor is! I'd willingly have given anyone £5 to take away that horse!"

I called him Eno, because the anxiety of riding him was liable to have much the same effect as a dose of salts. I never did cure him of his habits, though I did manage to come to a sort of agreement with him by which, after letting him have his own way for a bit, he would gradually come round and do what I wanted. Riding back through Hanney after a hunt one day, he suddenly leaped into the garden of the bakery. When I tried to persuade him to get out, he went on through the large doors into the bakehouse. I had to lie flat along his back with my arms round his neck to avoid being knocked off by the low beams. In the end he became lame, developed a ringbone arthritis of his off foreleg, and had to be put down.

Among my duties as Medical Officer to St Mary's Convent was attendance at a sanatorium for the girls of St Mary's School. The sanatorium was at a private house in Ormond Road, Wantage and was run by a Miss Scarell and Mabel Baldwin. Willie Dawson, the assistant doctor in the practice, who lived with me at Priory Road, and I often used to drop in there for a cup of tea. One day when we were having tea they mentioned that a new games mistress who was a good tennis player had just started at St Mary's, and suggested that we might like to come over for tennis one Sunday.

The following week there was a garden party and carnival in aid of the Wantage Hospital Building Fund – as I wrote earlier the hospital had cost more than its estimate, and although it had been in use for some time we had not finished paying for it. At the garden party we met Mabel Baldwin, who had with her the new games mistress, Ottilie, and her friend Flo Garrard, who also taught at St Mary's school. When the fete was over I walked back with the two young women, and invited them to join Willie and me at Priory Road for dinner that evening. They accepted, but it wasn't until we got home that I realised that I'd given Mr. and Mrs. Leach the day off for the carnival, and that the only food in the house was one pork pie! Dr Kennedy had taken away all his beautiful antique furniture, and I still had not furnished the dining room. So we ate at a card table in the sitting room, cheering up our solitary pie with a bottle of wine, and looking forward to Sunday, when Mabel Baldwin had invited us to tennis. I had rather a lot of calls to make that Sunday, and by the time I arrived the tennis had started, so I sat in a deck chair to watch. Ottilie was playing on the far court, and I noticed something special about her, a mixture of style and agility. I partnered her

*The family in the garden at Idris*

later in the mixed doubles, and felt a new confidence about my tennis. We won easily.

*Idris, Carbis Bay*

*On the beach at Carbis Bay*

We played together in many matches after that, and all too soon it was the end of term and St Mary's School broke up. That was the summer of 1930. As soon as the autumn term started I asked O. if she would like to come for a ride on the Downs, saying that I could borrow a horse for her from my friend Cyril Kent. (I have written O. because by that time I called her O. We decided that as we both had such frightful names, hers Ottilie and mine Vaughan, we would call each other O. and V.) ). O. agreed to come, but we never had that ride because I had a telephone call from Cambridge to say that my father was ill.

I drove to Cambridge in my Morris Cowley and found that my father had bronchitis, and that his heart was giving some cause for anxiety. I thought it best to bring both him and my mother back to Wantage, so that I could look after them. Over the next few days my father became weaker, and I could see that he was not getting better. On his last day he did not recognise me. He lay with his eyes fixed and staring, breathing rapidly with short, rasping breaths. Then, suddenly, all was quiet. Looking down

*Jennifer and Dick having their portraits painted in Arthur Haywood's gallery in St.Ives*

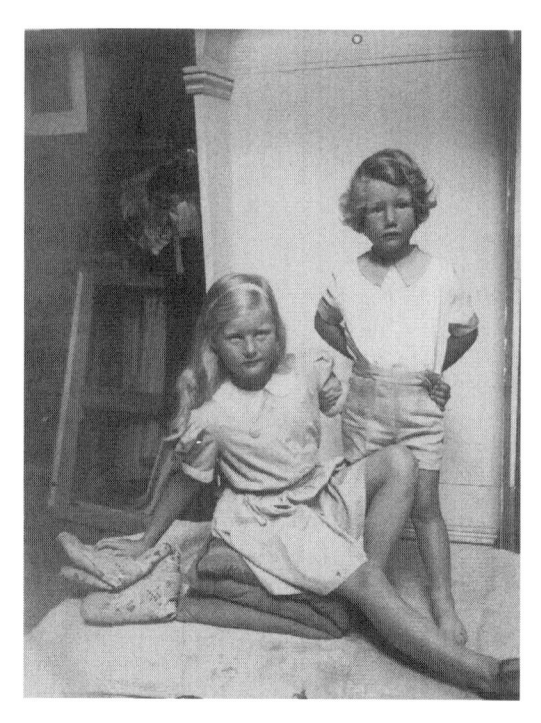

at his motionless, peaceful body I was overcome by an intense feeling of grief. What a brave struggle he had fought! I thought of his early days on the farm and his determination to go to Cambridge; then, when he had achieved a position in life, his partner had absconded with all the money.

How he and my mother had worked to pay back debts that were not of their making. I felt

*Jennifer and Dick feeding pigeons in Trafalgar Square*

both proud and humble as I stood there looking at him.

After the funeral I suggested to my mother that she might like to make her home at 2 Priory Road with me. She agreed, went back to Cambridge to collect her belongings, and sold Vale House for £600. She enjoyed living at Wantage. With her gentle charm and sense of humour she soon made many friends, and she would often come round with me on my calls.

*Married on 12th January 1932 at St. George's, Hanover Square*

O.'s father was a strange man. His father – her grandfather had been Headmaster of Dulwich College, and he told his son that he could become either a doctor or a lawyer. He chose medicine, but when it came to examinations after two years at Cambridge he simply signed his name, and walked out. He then went to Burma, where he joined the Bombay-Burma Teak Corporation, and spent the rest of his working life in Burma. On one of his leaves in England he had married, and taken his wife back to Burma. O. was born in Rangoon, as was her brother. The climate, however, was considered unsuitable for European children, so their mother brought them back to England. Her own home was in Germany, and she went to live there, leaving the children to go to school in England, and to spend their holidays with relatives.

When O.'s father retired he bought a cottage at St Ives, in Cornwall, and this was now O.'s home, where she went in the holidays from St Mary's. At Easter 1931 I suggested that my mother might like a touring holiday in the West Country, with our final destination St. Ives. We had a splendid time, visiting my mother's sister at Bristol, and old friends from Adelaide at Porlock. Eventually we arrived at the Tregenna Castle Hotel, between St. Ives and Carbis Bay.

I adored St. Ives as soon as I set eyes on it, and the artists' colony there fascinated me. Over the next few years I made many friends there, notably Arthur Hayward and John Parkes.

O.'s house had wonderful views across St. Ives Bay, and one could walk right down to the beach, across fields and along the cliffs. Nothing is more exhilarating than Cornwall in the spring, with its primrose banks and masses of other wild flowers. I loved every minute of it, and our holiday was a great success.

That summer O. and I played a great deal of tennis together, and shared some wonderful rides over the Downs. Our partnership on the tennis court had been so successful that I asked her if she would like it to continue into everyday life. She agreed, and in September we became engaged, fixing a date for our marriage in January 1932.

I had a one-third share in the practice, which I had bought for £6,000. While we were making arrangements for our wedding Dr Birt asked if I would like to make my share up to half. Naturally I wanted this, for it would put us on an equal footing in the practice, but it meant finding another £3,000. To contract such a debt on the eve of marriage needed thinking about. When I explained my difficulties to Birt, he said "Don't strain yourself, old chap. It's a good practice, and if you don't want it I can easily sell it to someone else." I was damned if I was going to have anyone else coming into the practice leaving me still a junior partner, so I set about raising a bank loan. The manager of my own bank said that he did not feel justified in advancing me so much money, so I put my problem to a hunting friend who was then manager of Barclay's Bank, Mr. Grainger. Old Grainger was a popular figure at local meets, always starting off in immaculate riding gear. But it was said of him that he was the horsiest man on foot and the footiest man on a horse – for his horsemanship did not match his outfit. After a few jumps he would usually have fallen off, to the detriment of his beautiful clothes. He was a good sort, however, listened to my story, and agreed to let me have the overdraft, so I was able to acquire my half-share in the practice, but I remained rather anxious at the thought of getting married with such a large overdraft hanging over me.

On 12, January 1932 O. and I were married at St George's Hanover Square. Although it was in the middle of winter, it was a lovely wedding, and a wonderful chance to meet all the family and catch up with family news. Uncle Will and Aunt Gwen arranged a reception for us at the Royal Institution and we had five days honeymoon at Brighton before returning to Wantage and the practice.

Later that year Dr Birt announced that he was going to retire. This meant more financial problems, because I had not had time to pay off my overdraft. But I was determined to keep the practice somehow, and our assistant, Willie Dawson, agreed to become a partner. For the next few years I worked harder than at any other time in my life. We had about 7,000 patients between the two of us, about half of them private patients, and the others on the panel or belonging to a club for medical treatment. State insurance in those days was compulsory only for wage-earners earning less than £5 a week (that, it must be remembered, was approaching a middle-class salary). Insured workers were entitled to medical treatment from the doctor who accepted them on what was called his "panel". They paid nothing for treatment, and the doctor was paid a per capita fee by the Government for them. That worked well enough as far as the wage-earner himself was concerned, but the scheme did not apply to his wife and family. They could obtain medical benefit by subscribing to various societies, but many poor women, hard put to it to make ends meet on their husbands' wages, could not find even the few pence a week needed to join a benefit society. That was the reason for the flood of gynaecological cases when the National Health Service was introduced, as women, who had sacrificed themselves for years for their families were at last able to go to a doctor without worrying about how their treatment was to be paid for. An alternative scheme, to which many people belonged (although there were still some who were either too poor or too feckless to join) was the Hospital Savings scheme. In our area this came under the Radcliffe Infirmary in Oxford. For 2d a week, or 4d to include a wife and an unlimited number of children, a patient was entitled to free treatment at either the Radcliffe, or the Wantage

*Priory Road*
*Self and mother, the March, and Jennifer*

hospital. Consultants gave their services free under this scheme, in return for being able to use hospital facilities for their private patients (who, of course, would also have to pay the hospital, according to their means).

Our practice extended to a radius of about nine miles around Wantage, the boundaries being roughly Faringdon, Lambourn, Chieveley (outside Newbury), Blewbury, Sutton Courtenay (just outside Abingdon), Marcham, Southmoor and Buckland. I had my own X-Ray plant, which I used at the surgery, charging one guinea an X-Ray. I did all minor (and some not so minor) surgery myself – tonsils, adenoids, hernias and appendectomies. Nowadays, when a GP diagnoses appendicitis he can telephone the Radcliffe in Oxford, telephone for an ambulance, and his part in things is accomplished in five minutes. Then, if I had a case of appendicitis I had to take the patient to Wantage Hospital in my car, arrange for an anaesthetist, operate to remove the appendix and look after the patient in hospital until he could be discharged, usually about a week later. This was undoubtedly satisfying from a medical point of view, but it made great demands on one's time.

I used to start work soon after 8 a.m. and seldom finished until nine o'clock at night. I hardly ever had a Sunday free, but I tried to save my more distant country calls as a kind of Sunday treat, on which I could take O. and my mother for the drive.

One call that I particularly enjoyed was visiting Maurice Reade, the farmer at Baulking Green. He suffered from high blood pressure, for which in those days we had no treatment except blood-letting. I used to draw off about a pint of blood from him, after which he would say, "Thanks, Doc. I feel a treat now." The blood would be drawn off into a pail, and he always insisted that it should be fed to his pigs!

I used to charge thirty shillings for removing tonsils and adenoids, and I recall one farm worker's approaching me to ask if I would operate on his three small boys at a special rate. I agreed to do all three for the price of one – thirty shillings – but he still thought that rather expensive. He belonged to the Hospital Savings scheme, so he had the alternative of going over to Oxford, where his sons could have the services of the consultant surgeon at the Radcliffe free. I pointed out to him, however, that the cost to the family in return bus fares would not be much less than thirty shillings. He went away to think about this and returned a few days later to say that the bus company had excursion fares to Oxford on Thursdays, and that the excursion fares would come to only twenty-five shillings. So I agreed to remove his sons' tonsils at excursion rates.

Collecting the tuppences for the hospital scheme was done by voluntary workers in a weekly door-to-door collection. The area was divided into collection districts, for each of which a voluntary worker would be responsible. O. used to collect from the Challow Road and Belmont district. She always went round on Mondays, because Monday was washing day, and the women would be sure to be at home. That gave her a good way of meeting my patients, and she was often able to help with their problems. Sometimes, if the washing had been done, O. would find her customers shelling peas or peeling potatoes when she called. O. would carry on with the shelling or peeling while the housewife went off to find her tuppence. Hospitals then, apart from the Workhouse infirmaries and some municipal hospitals in big towns, were supported entirely by voluntary subscriptions. That meant a constant need for fund-raising. O. was chairman of the Linen Guild, which was responsible for providing all the bedding for Wantage Hospital. We were always having whist drives, dances, or garden parties in aid of the Linen Guild. It is strange to recall now what a huge volume of wholly voluntary work was required for the upkeep of hospitals in Britain before the National Health Service.

I had one patient whom I simply could not persuade to enter hospital. She was an old lady living in a small thatched cottage, and she was seriously ill, feeling sick, running a fever, and suffering from increasing pain on the right side of her abdomen. I diagnosed an infected gall-bladder, and asked her to come into Wantage Hospital so that I could operate. She said "Do what you like to me, doctor, but I'm not going into any hospital. If you want to do anything to me, do it at home." Well, I had to operate. I sterilised my instruments by boiling them in the kitchen. I gave the patient a morphia injection as well as a local anaesthetic over the gall bladder, and as there was no electricity in the cottage I got the District Nurse to hold a torch for me while I worked. I evacuated pus from the infected bladder, and removed a quantity of gallstones, like small marbles. I left a tube to drain the wound, and came back rather apprehensively next morning. To my relief I found the old lady much improved. She handed me another gallstone, remarking "I found another of your balls in my bed."

We had no ambulance in Wantage until 1934, when Mr. Whitlam, who lived at Letcombe, presented one to the hospital. At about the same time the hospital benefited from another generous gift, from the father of a patient. The patient was Henry Dawson, the son of Dick Dawson, a well known trainer and farmer who lived at Fawley Manor. He was driving down Workhouse Hill when his car got out of control, hitting the bank and turning over. He was picked up unconscious and taken to Wantage Hospital. I examined him carefully and X-rayed his skull, but I could find no fracture. A week later he was still unconscious. Dick Dawson, his father, became increasingly worried, and I agreed to a second opinion. I called in a radiographer from the Radcliffe, but he could only agree with my findings. A few days after this, Henry Dawson regained consciousness, and he made a complete recovery. Dick Dawson was so grateful to the hospital that he bought a piece of land behind it to be available should an extension to the hospital be needed. That piece of land now carries the Health Centre attached to the hospital.

On 15, March 1934 our first child, Jennifer, was born at home at 2 Priory Road. All went well until a few days after O.'s delivery, when her temperature began to soar. There were no antibiotics then, and there was little I could do but give her aspirin. Her condition deteriorated, and I was desperately worried. I asked my friend Wyatt, the consultant at St Thomas's, to come down to see her, and he arranged for her to be admitted to the hospital. She travelled to London in a superb Rolls Royce ambulance that belonged to St Thomas's. O. was saved by the nursing and attention at St Thomas's. Her fever gradually subsided and at last she was able to come home.

My brother Stenie had a wonderfully kind nanny called Elsie to look after his children, and as they had really outgrown the need for a nanny, Elsie came to Wantage to look after Jennifer, and later our son Dick. Elsie was one of the kindest and sweetest people I have ever known, with an extraordinary influence over children: she could gain a child's confidence within a few minutes of meeting him. Elsie was to remain with us for 20 years, to become a much-loved member of the family.

Alice came over from Adelaide that summer, and with my brother Stenie and my mother we all went down to Cornwall. We had a narrow escape from disaster. Stenie and I had gone over to Kynance on a day that had been stormy, but had cleared. When we got down to the beach we decided to have a bathe. There were huge rollers crashing in from the Atlantic, which made our bathe wonderfully exhilarating. I could feel the powerful undertow, but I found that by digging my toes into the sand and using my hands as paddles I could stand against it. Suddenly I looked round and saw Stenie drifting out to sea. He kept his head, conserving his strength and just floating, but he continued to be carried out to sea, sinking out of sight in the trough of the waves. Mercifully he got into a current which was setting on shore, though he was still some way out. While I had been watching him helplessly, some holidaymakers on the beach had got hold of a line, and holding on to this I swam out to Stenie. He was very much exhausted, but I put the line and my arms round his waist, called to the people on the beach to heave, and they were able to drag us in. O. and my mother had watched the drama in acute anxiety from the top of the cliff.

O. continued to suffer abdominal pain, and in March 1938, when our son Dick was born, her old infection flared up again. Three months later, when she thought that she had got over it, she suddenly collapsed while playing tennis. The Wantage ambulance rushed her to the Radcliffe, where a huge abscess was found to have ruptured. Those were anxious days, but the abscess was drained and O. pulled through. The Wantage ambulance brought her home not so luxurious as St Thomas's Rolls Royce, but a homecoming that was a joy and infinite relief.

I tried to give myself one day off a week, which, when I could, I spent hunting. I could seldom get away early enough to start with the meet, so I got special permission for my groom to ride at the back of the field, and when I could leave my surgery I would set off to find the hunt by car. I used to do those morning surgeries with a pair of old trousers over my riding breeches, and wearing a sports jacket instead of a hunting coat. Looking for the hounds was a tricky business; sometimes I would fail to find them at all and drive home very cross with myself, while my groom went on with the hunting. But I got quite good at tracking the hounds, and learned signs to tell me whether they had passed this way or that. The behaviour of cows was often a reliable indicator: if cows are grazing peacefully with their heads down it is fairly certain that they have not recently been disturbed; if they stand looking in one direction it may mean that the hounds have passed by – they will always gaze in the direction that the hounds have gone. My day off was usually no more than part of a day off; as soon as I got home I would have a bath and change, and then set off on a round of evening visits to patients.

There were some entertaining characters in the hunting field. One was old Mrs. Aitken, who lived at Southmoor. She was the first woman to ride in an Old Berks Point-to-Point: she had studied all the old records, found that there was no rule actually forbidding women to ride, and duly entered, to the dismay of the hunt officials, who discovered that they had no power to refuse her entry. The course for that famous Point-to-Point was at Faringdon, and Mrs. Aitken hired a large marquee in which she gave a celebration lunch before her race. She was riding a big bay mare, and for a time she was leading the field, and looked all set to win. But the mare suddenly lost speed. Mrs. Aitken explained to me afterwards, "She was going marvellously, my old lady, but suddenly she came into season. When a lady is in a condition like that she can think of nothing else – her concentration on the race failed."

Mrs. Aitken's husband never rode himself, but he always drove his wife to meets in their old Ford car. He drove, and she sat in the back. One day he got to a meet, opened the door for his wife – and found that she wasn't there. He had been waiting in the car outside their home, heard the rear door slam, and driven off. What had actually happened was that Mrs. Aitken had forgotten her hat, and gone back to fetch it. There was another great excitement when Mrs. Aitken thought that she had bought a car at an auction, for what seemed a marvellous bargain price. It turned out that what she had in fact bought was a Boy Scout's outfit – the auctioneer had had his foot on the running board of a car, but he was selling the Boy Scout uniform. Mrs. Aitken always wore a ginger wig. It caught on a branch of a tree once when she was jumping the Rosy Brook, and it was quite a job to retrieve it inside her hat.

A number of army regiments stationed in places where there

was not much scope for riding used to ask hunts if they could ride over their country. We had one such request from the Fourth Dragoon Guards at Aldershot, and they used to join us quite often. One of our favourite events was a "Go as you please" race across country, and we invited the Guards riders to join in. Bob Pike of Lyford was very keen on this race, and offered to fix a course. He asked me to ride with the field, saying that as many of the other riders would be in strange country he felt that a Medical Officer ought to be at hand. At that time I had a marvellous mare called Heron. She had been given to me by the retiring MFH, Paget Stevenson, who explained that he liked to give things away during his lifetime so that he could see the pleasure his gifts gave.

Bob Pike's course lay between Denchworth and Baulking Green, and the race started from Honour's Farm. The first two fences were jumped easily, and then it was downhill to Denchworth Brook. On the far side of the brook was a fairly stiff cut-and-laid hedge, so that the horses would have to lift really high to clear the hedge as well as the brook. The whole field refused, and then refused again. I was riding with the field on Heron, but not really taking part in the race. When I saw the second refusal I put Heron at the brook and shouted to the others to follow. Heron was a most experienced hunter, and when they saw her clear the brook and the hedge the other horses all followed. We galloped past Blackacres Farm and crossed the road at a place where straw had been laid down for us. The Guards Colonel was in the lead, on a fine weight-bearing thoroughbred. We went on past Goosey, and then towards Rosy Brook. Here there was another difficult obstacle – a stream, with a tall post-and-rail fence, then a bank which one had to land on, to take off again immediately to clear the post-and-rails on the far side, and another stretch of water. It was here that Heron made her famous leap. She was as keen as mustard, and going so fast that she cleared the lot without landing halfway. The stewards measured it afterwards, and found that it was 34 ft.

O. was watching with Freddie Fox, the King's Jockey who lived at Letcombe. She thought it strange that Heron dropped her hind legs on the far side of the ditch, little realising that she had already jumped. O. and Freddie Fox drove on to watch the finish, and I kept going on Heron. I was really trying to hold her back, because it would have been a bit embarrassing if I won the race that I was supposed to be attending as a Medical Officer. But she was going so splendidly, and I was so wound up with excitement that I had to fight with myself as well as Heron. I am ashamed to say that those who did fall off didn't get much attention – I would shout "Are you all right, there?" but be out of earshot before I could get a reply. Freddie Fox saw that I was trying to hold back Heron, and he shouted to me "Come on Doc, or I'll have you reported to the stewards for pulling!" Fortunately the Colonel on his thoroughbred just managed to win, and we had a sumptuous luncheon in a marquee on Baulking Green.

That was almost the last of our peacetime occasions. Every day the radio blared with more and more dreadful outpourings from Hitler and soon England was at war again, for the second time in my lifetime.

# Chapter 10

# War Again

After the initial shock, the first months of war – the so-called phoney war – meant little to us in the country, except the wearisomeness of the blackout and the gradual disappearance from shops of one's favourite brands of anything.

We went down to Carbis Bay that autumn. I spent a morning in Arthur Hayward's gallery, discussing the merits of his latest oil colour, and then we retired next door to the Sloop Inn for a pint of beer. We were half listening to the lunch time news when my attention was caught by an announcement that the government needed at least 200 medical practitioners to volunteer for service in the RAMC to cope with the casualties at the front. When I got back to our cottage I wrote to the War Office, rather on the spur of the moment, offering to enlist. When we returned to Wantage after the holiday I told my partner, Willie Dawson, what I had done, and he was naturally anxious about the future of the practice.

After about a week I got a letter from the War Office telling me to report to Millbank, in London, to be interviewed and to have a medical inspection. The interview went well enough, but then we were told to take off all our clothes and stand nude in a straight line. Most men there were young newly qualified doctors, but there were a few of us seasoned old general practitioners, trying to look dignified but feeling very naked.

A few days after I got home I heard that I had been accepted. I was advised to get a locum for the practice, and that I should be sent for in a few days. But things then reached rather a stalemate state in France with both sides looking at one another. The ways of the War Office are traditionally odd and just as the Germans launched their powerful offensive which ended in our getting out by the skin of our teeth at Dunkirk, I had another letter saying that they would not need as many doctors as they had thought at first, and would I stand by as a reserve in case of need? As I was paying my locum £20 a week, he very soon had to go. In fact it was more than two years before I was sent for and told to report to the Crookham Barracks at Aldershot, where I would join the Royal Army Medical Corps and receive the standard pay of 19s11d a day.

The whole family came over to see me into Crookham Barracks. We had a farewell meal in a pub in Aldershot, which was a great treat because rationing had started, but hotels and restaurants did not have to adhere quite so closely to the ration book as the rest of us and we were able to have a good feed without giving up our precious points and coupons.

It was strange to go back into community life again. School, the 1914-18 war and Cambridge seemed very distant, yet now, at my time of life, I returned to sleeping in a dormitory. Next day we were given all the injections going – smallpox, typhoid, cholera, yellow fever and tetanus – all at once, and that same evening, in true army fashion when we all had fevers, we were given an intelligence test. I was horrified to find how slow we older men were, and a bit mortified when the doctor who came top of the intelligence test turned out to be a young woman. We were told (and I sympathised) that Guards officers refused to take intelligence tests.

We spent about a month at Aldershot, attending a host of army lectures on all kinds of boring (but I suppose useful) subjects, such as how to wash one's hands in the tropics. We then received postings. My companions were a bit depressed to be posted as far afield as Glasgow and Edinburgh. I sympathised, but then my own posting came – to Scapa Flow in Orkney!

It was a miserable trip to Orkney. We left Euston in the morning in a slow troop train, and were pushed into sidings whenever an express came by, so that we eventually arrived in Perth two hours late. We had been promised a meal in a hotel at Perth, and we were all famished, having had nothing to eat since morning. As we were so late the hotel would not give us a meal. The Salvation Army came to the rescue. It ran an all-night hostel for down and outs, and fed us all with tea and buns. We had a happier experience at Thurso the next morning when we went for breakfast at the Commercial Hotel. A vast meal was set before us, and there was food the like of which we had not seen since before the war: porridge and cream, bacon, eggs and sausages. And there was no question of ration cards.

At Scapa Flow I was posted to a hospital carrier called the *Dinard* which had been stationed there for some months. In peacetime she had been a Southern Railway cross-channel steamer. Most of our hospital carriers had been cross-channel or Irish packet boats, whose shallow draft and speed made them particularly useful for combined operations for the invasion of enemy territory from the sea.

Our *Dinard* was about 2,200 tons, with a speed of about 22 knots. The dining saloons and lounges had been stripped of all tables and chairs, and replaced by rows of cots. Each cot, rather like a baby's cradle, was pivoted at the head and foot so that it could be fixed stationary in calm weather but allowed to swing free in rough conditions to counteract the rolling of the ship. There were five wards, with a reception ward in the stern, and the operating theatre was to be in the middle of the ship where the movement was the least. On the boat deck, suspended on the davits, were six ambulance boats. These were flat-bottomed barges able to carry six stretcher cases and twelve walking wounded. The davits were electrically operated, which enabled the ambulance boats to be lowered quickly. Once our troops had landed on a beach, the boats were run up on the sands, nose first.

There were several hospital carriers anchored then in Scapa Flow. We received the casualties from the convoy ships which were going from Scapa Flow to Russia. Any surgical case would go to a carrier which had an operating theatre; as we then had no operating theatre, we would take medical cases from the convoys, or from the personnel based at Scapa Flow. When we had a full load of casualties, 250, we would ferry them to the large hospital at Aberdeen.

The *Dinard* went to war with the same captain and crew who had once taken trippers across the Channel – the Southern Railway in battledress, as it were. There were four of us on the medical staff. The surgeon, Sid Green, was a man in his thirties, who had his surgery fellowship, and who had a very fast, clear-thinking brain, with the theoretical side of surgery at his fingertips. We got on well together, and he gave me great encouragement. I had probably had quite a lot more practical experience than he had, but I was careful not to appear too pushing, and only gave an opinion when asked. We had an anaesthetist Captain Montgomery Brown (Alex) who worked in Glasgow; he has been a good friend and we have kept in touch to this day. Then there were two of us who were glorified housemen, or General Duties Officers Coombes and myself. I liked Coombes, though he was liable to get upset by little things which I thought unimportant; if I beat him at a game of chess, for instance, it could upset him for a whole evening. We were soon on Christian name terms, and as nobody liked my name Vaughan, I was rechristened Bob.

The general attitude to authority was markedly different in

the Second World War from what it had been in the First. At Woolwich Barracks in 1914 we had imagined ourselves to be knights in shining armour, preparing to defend our Fatherland, and we felt infinite respect for the rows of medals displayed by veterans of the Boer War. In the Second World War, if one had a First War medal, one took pains to hide it, lest one should be classed as an old has-been. Life at Scapa had a pretty deadly monotony. There was routine work and very little else. Twice a week we were allowed a trip into Stromness for tea organised by the Church of Scotland in Nissen huts. I was better off than most of my mates in that I could always keep myself occupied with my sketchbook. I used to go for long walks along the coast from Stromness, enjoying the wild, romantic scenery, and watching the eider ducks and puffins that thronged the low-lying islands. On a still day there was an awe-inspiring quietness, broken only by the chattering of the oyster-catchers.

One major excitement was a visit from a floating concert hall, an entertainment ship which came from Scotland. This put on a film show, and each ship's company was allowed to visit it in turn. When our turn came we scrambled excitedly into the *Dinard*'s boat for our treat. We had to go about 2 miles to the floating cinema, and on the way a big destroyer passed, drenching us with her wash. Being December, it was very cold. Anyway, our morale stayed high, but the film was a bit of a flop. Halfway through the manager came out and stopped it, saying that he was very sorry, but he had got the reels muddled, and had shown the second reel first. So from the end of the film we went back to the beginning, seeing the story leading up to all the things we had already seen. At least it was a change from the routine.

I was bothered by the waste of time in being stuck at Scapa, with very little to do and the prospect of being posted, because of my age, to some depot where I would have endless medical examinations and fitness parades for enlisting soldiers – work which was not only intensely boring, but a waste of my own capabilities. I decided that the one thing which would take me out of this predicament, and allow me to take part in the war in a more worthwhile role, was to improve my qualifications. With this in mind I got hold of my medical textbooks and started working about two or three hours a day, with a view to taking my fellowship of surgery if the opportunity ever arose. With an FRCS after my name I should be able to do more of the surgery in which I was really interested.

And then came the break I had been waiting for. The male nurse on the *Dinard* who acted as ward master came to my sick parade, saying that he had a belly ache, and was feeling sick. As soon as I examined him I realised that he had appendicitis. As we had no operating theatre I signalled to the Naval Floating Hospital, saying that I was bringing over a surgical case. We lowered the old ward master, whose condition was deteriorating, into an open boat and set off for the naval ship. I had been told by the Captain of the *Dinard* that I was to stand to attention in the bows of the boat, to show that I was in charge. This was not only ridiculous when I had a very sick man to look after, but also very difficult in the December swell.

When we reached the naval ship I explained the case to the Captain, who seemed rather embarrassed. The ship's surgeon, he said, had just had a nervous breakdown; could I possibly cope with the ward master if he gave me a scalpel and the run of the theatre?

I took out the ward master's appendix, with the navy watching to see how the army performed. I realised how important this was to me, but all went well. It was a gangrenous appendix, but I got it out in about 20 minutes, and the old chap did very well.

Soon afterwards I did a locum for the surgeon on the naval shore base, which I enjoyed. The surgeon had been an orthopaedic specialist, and I was careful not to try to cope with any job outside my range.

I had a week's leave at Christmas, taking the boat to the mainland at Scrabster, having a huge feed at the Commercial Hotel in Thurso, and trundling down south in the train. I had arranged to meet O. at Paddington before taking the train to Wantage, and we had a quick meal at the station buffet. How different from Thurso! All we could get at Paddington was scrambled eggs and the mess was made either from powdered eggs, or from those disgusting tinned Chinese eggs which were available during the war.

On arriving at Wantage I felt very guilty about my months of idleness at Scapa Flow. The practice was busy, and O. had been struggling to keep our large house going. What a change from the early days of our married life when we had a cook, a gardener, and housemaids! Now O. had to do everything herself as well as cope with an evacuee whose family were coming for Christmas. Although it was the middle of winter, O. had been frantically weeding the tennis court, and trying to get it cut, with the children adding extra force by towing the lawnmower with a piece of rope. They knew how upset I would be if I came home to find the tennis court, with all its happy memories, a hay field. This was, indeed, the war effort on the home front.

I returned to Scapa Flow in the New Year of 1943 to be met with the news that we were to sail soon to the Clyde for refitting, and to be equipped with an operating theatre. The *Dinard* was also to be given extra fuel tanks, to cope with longer voyages. We had a beautiful trip through the Western isles during early spring, spoiled only by the thought of war.

Our stay in the Clyde gave me a wonderful chance to get on with the practical side of my study of surgery. Sid Green knew how important it was to me to be recognised as a graded surgeon, and he gave me every encouragement. I needed access to pathology labs where I could see slides and specimens, so I went to Edinburgh, visited the university medical school, and found someone who would give me tutorials. This was an enormous help, though I was hampered by the wartime closure of some of the laboratories.

I sat for the FRCS exam just before we were due to leave the Clyde. I passed the written paper, but failed the practical. I had no regrets, though, because without the time I had spent studying I should not have been able to cope with all the surgery I was to meet later in the war.

By June, all the reconstruction had nearly been completed. We had our smart operating theatre amidships, where the movement of the ship was least. The operating table was fixed to the floor with chains (though even these broke during a violent storm in the Mediterranean later, dropping the unconscious patient on the floor of the theatre). We also had a bar beneath the table, under which we could put our toes to brace ourselves against the action of the ship. As things turned out, however, during rough weather Sid Green had to be further steadied by a nurse standing behind him, holding on to his waist. We had hoped for a water distillation plant, which would enable us to obtain fresh water from the sea, but this was considered by the authorities as too expensive. That was a miserable economy, as we realised later when we learned the hard way what an inconvenience and anxiety lack of fresh water could be.

Our ideas as to the exact part in the war we were to play were rather hazy, but as the *Dinard* was nearing completion we were all assembled in the officers' lounge for a short address and the usual fine words by those in higher command, to make sure that our morale did not flag. We were told that we would take part in the allied invasion of Sicily and Italy when, as Churchill had said, we struck at "the soft underbelly of Europe". We would follow about a day behind the landing of the troops, picking up the wounded as they were brought down to the beaches. Our task, we were told, would not only help the wounded, but raise the morale generally, as the fighting soldiers would know that if they were wounded there would be help at hand. It was pathetic later to discover how we were regarded as a heaven on earth – or rather the sea – by men who had, perhaps, been lying on the beaches at Anzio with appalling wounds for a day or so, hearing shells all round them and unable to move.

Now that we had our operating theatre we embarked a young matron, and about half a dozen nurses. I felt rather sorry for the girls when they arrived. They had volunteered for active service, probably expecting to be on some shore base, with a lot of charming army officers; but now they were to be whisked into the heat of the fighting in a ship, with their only previous experience of the sea perhaps a fishing trip during seaside holidays.

When the matron heard what was expected of her nurses, her first reaction was the thought of their modesty. She knew, she said, what it would be like when we had a lot of wounded on board – all those men would be lying sunning themselves on deck looking up at the nurse's open drawers Well, it did not turn out to be quite like that. But the matron did put all her girls into neat slacks.

In the week before we sailed O. came up and stayed at Gourock. The Clyde was certainly looking spectacular, with all the shipping waiting for repairs, or waiting for posting.
Historical note:
In November 1942 the British won the Battle of Alamein and drove the Germans and Italians out of Libya. Then came the Allied landing in North Africa, and the pincer move which cleared Tunisia. Tunis itself was occupied in May 1943 and two months later the Allies landed in Sicily. This was the background of events that brought the *Dinard* and her little company of doctors, nurses, RAMC personnel and ex-Channel service crew to the Mediterranean.

# Chapter 11

# Hospital Ship

We left the Clyde on June 25, 1943, reached Gibraltar on June 30, and a week later sailed for Bizerta. As far as I could, I kept a diary of my service on the *Dinard*. This was written at odd moments, often under stress, and, of course, without knowing anything of the main course of the war, except what was going on immediately around us. Nevertheless, my diary is a firsthand record of one aspect of one chapter of the war, and, as such, some extracts may be of interest.

NOTE  Paragraphs in italics were added by the author in 1972.

June 26  Arrived Falmouth about 4 p.m., marvellous evening, glassy water. Bathed off the ship while oiling. No shore leave much to everyone's disappointment. Orders received to sail to Gibraltar at 10 p.m. Left Falmouth on a glorious evening with strong lights and shade. Uneventful journey through Bay of Biscay in company with *St. David*, *St. Julian* and *St. Andrew*. The *Dinard* leading.

June 27  Passed by eighteen Flying Fortresses, ten on one side and eight on the otherside flying low. Flight of Mosquitoes pass us in the evening at deck level. Glorious sunshine.

*Photograph of self and a chum. Have sketched in the impression of a horse*

June 29 Passed St. Vincent with the lighthouse and old monastery shining white in the afternoon sun.

June 30 Falmouth to Gibraltar 1,054 miles. Up early on deck as we passed the Straits of Gibraltar with a view of Tangiers in the morning light. Anchored in the harbour of Gibraltar about a quarter of a mile from the Spanish shore – a glorious sunny morning. Oiled early and had a bathe. Went ashore in intense heat with Col., Cap. and Brown and bought tropical kit. Incessant depth charges against sticky bomb merchants all night.

*We just managed to reach Gibraltar with our fuel and fresh water supplies. It was very hot and Gibraltar was bristling with fortifications. Guy Shepherd, whose parents lived at The Ham in*

*The Dinard after renovation*

*Wantage, was an officer stationed on the Rock so we had some good times together – though I got severely sunburned. We used to be able to get a jeep to go around the far side of the island and bathe. I was very amused one morning because his adjutant had left the window of the office open as it was so hot and several monkeys had swarmed in during the night and pulled out all the drawers and filing cabinets – flinging papers in all directions and covering them with excreta.*

July 6   Went ashore and climbed the rock in intense heat and talked to air gunners on the summit and watched the salvage of a Liberator that fell into the sea with General Sikorsky and his daughter – pilot in Gibraltar hospital.

*At the end of the week we received orders to proceed to the N African port of Bizerta which was opposite Sicily and close for us to follow in the wake of the Sicilian invasion.*

July 8   Left Gibraltar at 8 a.m. with orders for Bizerta, 757 miles.

July 10   Arrived Bizerta – uneventful at 9 a.m. Heavy swell last night kept most people awake. Went ashore in barge. All dock area littered with wreckage of ships, planes and debris – stiff breeze. Coming and going of destroyers into harbour. Allied invasion of Sicily at 3 a.m.

7 p.m. two King George V battleships, 4 destroyers and 2 cruisers passed steaming eastwards at great speed. Heavy firing from air-raid over Tunis. Difficulty in obtaining water delayed our departure from 4.30 to 11 p.m. The Germans connected the main sewage into the water supply of Bizerta before evacuating the town. Orders to proceed to the S.E. coast of Sicily.

12.20 (midnight) Steaming at full speed under a half moon, very bright. Turning eastward out of Bizerta no lights on the ship. Final survey of reception ward to deal with all emergencies – finished revision of amputation. Had 2 whiskies with the Col. and shall turn in fully clad to face the day tomorrow when the medical and surgical staff will be put to the test which I hope will justify the long months of inactivity.

July 11   5 a.m. Passed Pantellaria. 9 a.m. Sicily in sight. Close into shore. Licata was first town located, covered by pall of smoke. Ships of all descriptions standing off. Tank landing craft in flames formed effective smokescreen. Sailing east along coast, further landings taking place by U.S. troops under cover of heavy naval bombardment from cruisers or destroyers – tankers and store ships lying further out to sea. First shell burst near *Dinard* persuaded all to don their tin hats. Fighter screen overhead continuous.

Arrived at our destination off Pachino, a sandy shore showing up white in brilliant sunlight with low land behind covered with farms and olive trees and a range of hills about 5-6 miles inland. 1st Canadians have effected a landing and clouds of dust and smoke can be seen on roads leading from the coast. Tank landing craft and L.S.T. still pouring vehicles on to the beach. Destroyers and cruisers standing by. We anchor alongside a monitor with her 15" guns trained on the shore. The *David* (*St David*, another hospital ship) picking up casualties from the beaches in her ambulance barges – casualties very light, and so far we have not been called on. A choppy sea is obviously making the work of the ambulance craft very difficult. Italian and German forces said to be holding the heights inland. 7p.m. flight of dive bombers attacking our forward troops. Terrific barrage laid on by every ship, the *Monitor* suddenly opening fire, nearly splitting our ear drums. Squadron of Spitfires appeared out of the sky and all quietened down. 8 p.m. L.C.T. and L.S.T. setting sail, some filled with prisoners. Heavy smokescreen covers their departure and fills our throats with nauseating fumes.

July 12   5 a.m. Dawn breaking. Hostile aircraft made attacks on our ships N and S of Cape Passero. Patrol destroyers immediately laid smoke. Once again terrific barrage of shell, tracers from pompoms and flak. 9 a.m. Minesweepers busy clearing the sea. *St David* took on and treated 129 casualties – wounds excised and sprinkled with penicillin, sulphonamide not being considered very effective. Col. Fraser on board wishes us to try Proflavine as experiment, and to decide the most effective. Abdominal perforating wounds left.

Landed on Sicily myself at 4.30 p.m. edge of sand, rocky. Inspected beach dressing station, a canvas shelter to which casualties have been brought by stretcher and returning lorries. Canadians have advanced inland about 4 miles. Bulldozers have forged a level track through sand. This has been covered with wire netting and canvas. Incessant stream of lorries, Bren gun carriers and light tanks using this roadway on to main roads inland. Men on beaches have cut slits in sand and covered them with pampas grass (like thin bamboo) to ward off the sun. E.M.O. has a shelter of pampas grass which he erected soon after landing. Alongside this was a pile of land mines collected by the Sappers. L.C.T. landing vehicles on a rough ramp. Casualties being conveyed from beach shelters into hospital water ambulance. Heat intense. Men black and sweating in the sun dragging vehicle ammunition ashore while destroyers, corvettes, frigates and monitors guard the sea and sky. Montgomery's troops 51st Highland division and Independent Brigade having landed N of Cape Pessaro which is about 1 mile N of us, have captured Syracuse which is a good port and will make our work much easier.

*The landings take place at dawn as it was considered the trickiest time for the enemy to see our troops, with the troops being able to find their way. Each division would have its own M.O. and stretcher bearers which was an uncomfortable task, having very distressing injuries to cope with and having little more than a first aid set and morphia. They worked under very difficult conditions with the enemy gunfire and shells exploding round them the whole time. I had great admiration for their guts and coolness – and of course many were killed. They would collect the wounded and set up temporary first aid posts and digging slit trenches on the beach, covering them with pampas grass or corrugated iron if it was available. There they would wait until we came with the hospital carriers and would take a batch back to the ship.*

July 13   Not much sleep for us. Heavy aerial attack and bombings of our positions. Every ship opening fire in an intense barrage, from 11 to 1 a.m., starting again at 4.15 a.m. Once again our destroyers made smoke, comforting but suffocating.

*As a hospital ship we were technically neutral and would not be bombed or fired on by shore batteries. In the early morning if we were with other shipping the enemy might not be able to see our white paint and red cross so we would have to take our chance with the other shipping. If we were steaming through the open sea we were allowed to put on all our lights so we looked like a floating Gin Palace but when we were within three miles of our own shipping we would have to turn all our lights off. We had a visit that morning from the A.D.M.S. and the matron asked if we could steam slightly further from the shore at night as we were still waiting for our turn to pick up casualties.*

July 14   Quiet night for a change. Aerial activity and gunfire farther N and inland. Ships leaving this beach as advance inland penetrates deeper. Water shortage acute, thanks to authorities at home not furnishing us with apparatus for distilling from sea. No water ashore though we could get buckets and casks of wine. The *David* left yesterday for Sousse. The *Julian* (*St. Julian*, another hospital ship) now taking on patients. Visit *Julian* this morning and examine some cases. Most have been treated by surgical unit ashore. Compound supracondylar fracture of femur involving joint. Compound fracture of humerus with loss of tissue in radial nerve. Perforating wounds of abdomen and haematuria – wounds treated with sulphonamide, vaseline gauze and P.O.P. to extremities.
2.30 p.m. Receiving oil and water from destroyer *Brecon*. Their distiller can produce 1½ tons per hour and we are short of 70 tons so we shall still be short. We have a little water (half basin full) in morning to wash with but we have to use that for the rest of the day, using it for washing up, etc. Went over destroyer armed with six 4in guns, twin cannon 20 mm AA (like Spitfires are armed with) and "Chicago piano" pompoms, which fire tracers. Transmitter station like a furnace, with 10 men and machinery in a place size of my cabin. Heard that Americans had the stickiest time west of this near Licata. They were counter-attacked by 2 German divisions 500 yds from shore. Battleships,

cruisers and destroyers put down barrage and Yanks beat them back.

8 p.m. Orders received to proceed up the east coast of Sicily. Perfect night, with marvellous moon, oily sea and stiflingly hot. Anchored about 10 p.m. 5 miles S of Syracuse. Then the fun started. Flares were dropped over our ships to add to the brilliant moon. We all felt lit up like actors on a stage. AA from shore and ships opened up with a terrific barrage and till 1 a.m. it was hell let loose. The poor old *Dinard* rattled and rocked under deluge of bombs, machine guns and cannon. Three planes brought down quite close to the ship and are still burning, and so to bed. Heard that a circular torpedo was dropped last night which went round and round among the ships but luckily hit none. (Glad we did not know.)

July 15   Embarking casualties from 8 a.m. coming out in tank landing craft and invasion barges, also our ambulance barges, from country north of Pachino. Most of these are due to German paratroops that came down between 51st Division and the coast, hence our sudden move to this area. 250 on board by 2 p.m. Some treated already on shore by A.D.S. Heat terrific, everyone working stripped to waist – lower wards like furnaces – operating theatre like a Turkish bath in spite of extractor fan. Ship full, and left Pachino at 7.30 p.m. en route to Tripoli. Pump jammed in engine delayed us two hours. Great relief to move out of stifling heat and get sea breeze to say nothing of missing the aerial attack that seems to start every night at dusk.

*The wounded would be picked up from the beaches by our ambulance boats which would hold about sixteen stretcher cases and a quantity of sitting patients. The boats would be run up onto the beaches, and when full the powerful engines would be put in reverse and they would make their way back to the Dinard as quickly as possible.* When they reached the Dinard they would be winched upwards by the davits till their deck was opposite the Dinard's boat deck and the wounded would be unloaded.

It used to be my job to stand in the boat deck and receive the wounded and to sort them to various wards according to the severity of their condition; one of the sisters would give an injection against tetanus and those in severe pain would be given morphia.

When all the patients were loaded the chief skill was determining our priorities when a team of five medical officers would have to treat some 250-300 casualties in a few hours and we would have to work in great concentration lest we missed some case whose life might be saved by some simple first aid measure. Our chief concern was the resuscitation of those who had lost a lot of blood or were still bleeding – particularly those with concealed bleeding in the chest or abdominal cavity with a torn liver or spleen. Those whose injuries needed more lengthy complicated surgery would be made comfortable and wait for the larger hospitals in N. Africa where they could be operated on in better conditions. A perforating abdominal wound for instance could mean three to four hours work while we sorted through every inch of the bowel finding perhaps eight holes where the bullet went through successive loops of the bowel. So all we would do was increase the size of the point of entry and shake in some penicillin powder, leaving the repair to be done a few hours later when we reached North Africa.

We were anxious to get out to sea as soon as possible as the ship was stiflingly hot and the enemy action uncomfortably close. To our horror we had a message from the engine room that one of the water pumps which cooled the diesel engines was out of action and the first engineer was frantically trying to repair it. It takes great guts to keep a cool head in the bottom of a ship near enemy action when one knows that a direct hit and you will be the first to go down. After about half an hour I was joined on deck by the 1st engineer with sweat pouring off him, partly from the heat and physical energy and partly from the anxiety, and he said the 2nd engineer had relieved him.

*After what seemed like an eternity with the Dinard floating helplessly the engines throbbed into life again and with great relief we moved out of the stifling heat and away from the enemy action en route for Tripoli to unload our wounded.*

*The heat was intense in that July of 1943. Not only had we to contend with the battle casualties but malaria, dysentery and jaundice were taking a heavy toll on our men. Those nights when every porthole had to be closed and the ships blacked out completely lest we proved a temptation to marauding aircraft made the ship an inferno. On that twelve hour crossing we would be working all night either in the operating theatre or setting up blood transfusions for those who had severe blood loss. All the same it was very frustrating how little we were able to do at the time – and our job was really only patching up the worst cases until they reached N. Africa, and I could not help thinking our chief tool was probably injection of morphia to dull the pain and numb the anxiety. We reached the coast of N. Africa the next day.*

July 16 Noon, steaming along at 16 knots under blue sky and deep blue sea. Expecting to see Tripoli coast any moment. 1.30 land about 10 miles off – glaring yellow of Western Desert unmistakeable – with shipping and smoke to the west, which must be Tripoli harbour. 4 p.m. waiting for E.M.U. to disembark wounded. Harbour littered with sunken ships, some with only mast and funnels showing. Three sunk just at entrance to block approach. 7 large hospital ships in. Magnificent looking city of towers and minarets and square-faced buildings with flat roofs, all shining brilliantly with palm trees silhouetted in rows against them in the sunlight. Heat, and everyone dripping. We feel quite old and tested warriors now. A.D.M.S. came on board. Patients embarked on Z ship like a tank landing craft manned by Swazi pioneer corps, grand looking chaps with broad felt hats. The engineers of the craft were Indians who knelt down on a board to pray to Allah quite oblivious of everything. Went ashore with Cols. Brown and Green with A.D.M.S. who sent us for a drive round in his car. Visited 47th General Hospital, an Italian hospital captured complete with X-ray equipment etc. as a going concern. Had a fine view from the top across the fertile belt to the desert beyond. Typhus, and brothels all out of bounds to troops. A.D.M.S. told us of casualties to hospital ships in Sicilian landing. The *Telambra* bombed and sunk 30 miles from Sicily on the night before last. The *Dorsetshire,* bombed but not sunk, is expected into this harbour tonight but travelling slowly. Most of *Telambra* personnel and patients saved by life jackets. They were simply pushed over the side as there was no time for boats. Lights on the life jackets attracted a destroyer who rescued most of them. Both these ships were travelling fully illuminated at night - O.C. of the hospital ship *Abba* (Lloyd-Williams who was at Thomas's with me) told us they saw a red light glowing in the sea and steamed towards it. Found it was the light on the life jacket of a Canadian pilot. He had attacked the plane which was bombing the *Telambra* and fired a burst into the bomb rack at such close range that the explosion disintegrated his own plane; no sign was found of his observer. Another hospital ship (name not known) reported bombed. (NOTE This was the *Derbyshire*)

*A couple of days later we left for Italy with orders to proceed to Syracuse as the advancing allies were pushing the Germans further up Sicily. We had a very unpleasant experience as we steamed unsuspecteing into the harbor which we thought was Syracuse and were practically within hailing distance of the shore when four heavy bombs dropped close to our stern sending up sprays of water and a destroyer sends frantic Morse signals to us that we are north of Augusta and about to enter a port which is in enemy hands. It makes me sweat to this very day to think how close we were to disaster like a mouse with its nose about to snatch the cheese from the trap, drawing its head back just before the spring snaps down. I suppose, though, one was expecting a lot from the navigation of the ship. We had been creeping up the coast where there had been very little in the way of landmarks or lights as the dawn was breaking and poor old Dinard in peacetime had only had to go backwards and forwards from Dover to Calais – or at the most from Newhaven to Dieppe, till she could make the trip blindfolded.*

July 18   Left Tripoli at 9.30 a.m. steaming eastwards as far as Homs with orders for Syracuse.

July 19   8.30 a.m. Distant shore of Sicily appears out of the morning mist. 9 a.m. As we draw closer we see a town flanked by hills to the south. Suddenly 4 heavy bombs dropped close on our stern sending the water high into the air. Destroyer makes signal to us that we are N of Augusta! Old *Dinard* makes such an acute turn to the south that the ship trembles like an old lady faced by a bull in a field. We beat it southward ignominiously, with smoke belching from our funnels. Enter Syracuse harbour. A most fascinating old town, with high walls rising as a bastion from the sea. Fine harbour crowded with ships, loading stores, ammunition vehicles. A sunken hospital ship shows only her funnels with Red X above water. Two little boys row out in a boat loaded with lemons which they trade for chocolate, bread and cigarettes. Won't take money, they seem starving.

July 20   2 a.m. What a shambles! Having loaded with wounded at Syracuse we just managed to weigh anchor and escape from the harbour before the evening onslaught started. Every cot, every seat and floor space covered with men dirt grimed, black with the sun, Englishmen, Scotsmen, Canadians, Italians, Germans (prisoners of war), but most of them asleep with the sweat pouring from them. To avoid attracting notice from marauding aircraft we travel without lights until we are at least 30 miles from Sicily. Then the Red X and green lights come on, and full steam is ordered. One man asked to speak to me. He turns out to be Sir Ralph Glyn's chauffeur from Ardington. We are bound for Sousse and hope to arrive about 2 p.m. The shock of us nearly falling into enemy hands as well as being bombed was so great that I have to treat old "P to windward" for his nerves today.

*I remember that evening well. I was sitting in my cabin when there was a knock on the door. I opened the door and one of my fellow officers who we called Piss to Windward was standing there trembling all over and hardly able to speak. I am afraid the nickname we gave him is a naval one for a chap who is unable to undertake even a simple task without it going wrong. I felt sorry for "P to windward", some people mentally are unable to stand up to enemy action. In the First World War they would be shot for cowardice – I was more understanding and gave him half a grain of Phenobarbitone to settle him down for the night as he was in such a nervous state after the day's intense activity. We reached the N. African port of Sousse the next morning.*

July 21   Went alongside the quay to disembark all the patients. Sousse an attractive old town which has been heavily bombed, and all round the water front is a heap of ruins. Green discovered that his old Colonel was at a C.C.S. about 7 miles inland. We went out on a lorry which was going that way to a Field Hospital. Interesting to see the brown tents of the C.C.S hidden in an olive grove. Most of the staff sleeping out under small mosquito nets. Had bully beef and a mug of strongly brewed tea for dinner. Green brought the old man a bottle of whisky, and we had a tot before we left. Walked back across country, stone dust and thorny bushes. Wind was so hot that it felt as if it were smothering one. Eventually got on to the main road to Sousse as dusk was falling

– following the tracks made by the 8th Army in their advance. White with dust by the time we got back to the ship at 11 p.m. Up at 7 a.m. and bathed from the beach. Quite a novelty. Now at 11 a.m. we are oiling from a tanker out about half a mile from shore. 1 p.m. up with the "hook" and away for Sicily once more. Heard that one Field Ambulance complete with gliders was dropped into the sea just short of Sicily.

*This distressed us very much. This was a beautifully equipped unit which had a team of doctors and nurses who were to be towed well over the land by the Americans and then the glider would release the heavy hawser and it would drop down and be left dangling on the towing hook of the American plane. In this instance things did not go as planned. When the American pilot was faced with the barrage of fire on the Sicilian coast he got the breeze up, let his end free and the heavy hawser pulled the nose of the glider straight down into the sea killing everybody.*

*The pattern continued for the next few weeks, picking up casualties from Syracuse and using the hospital at Sousse to disembark them.*

July 22   Syracuse harbour again by 9 a.m. Sea like a duck pond and stiflingly hot. We send our water ambulance ashore by 10 a.m. and start to bring back the casualties; the 8th Army having pushed on between Augusta and Catania and meeting with strong German resistance. One Commando Lieut. told me that they were pushed on into Catania to make a nuisance of themselves and he thought the main troops were never coming. After 2 days and nights fighting with no sleep, the Durham Light Infantry arrived. By that time he had only 5 men left but the Col. of the D.L.I. asked him to hold their flank. So they held it, until he was wounded and the remaining 5 men were replaced by a company. Another fellow we have operated on tonight escaped from a tank which was set alight by a direct hit, burst into flames and he alone escaped with burns (the others were roasted alive). Great difficulty in supplying and relieving the forward troops, who are getting completely exhausted. Our ship completely loaded with casualties lying on stretchers on the deck, in deck chairs, on settees in the smoke room. Some bad chest cases, one with urinary and faecal fistula from right loin. One with penetrating wound below pericardium with complete paraplegia looks as if he will die tonight. Several cases from an ammunition ship that blew up in Augusta harbour.

*I learnt one interesting fact about the treatment of leg injuries. I remembered from the days of my physiology that when a limb is amputated during an accident the main arteries to the leg will suddenly go into spasm from the shock and so save the person's life by minimising the blood loss. Now a blood vessel which has had a severe shock without necessarily being cut will act in the same way, and go into spasm. We sometimes picked up a man with shrapnel wound in the leg and his leg would be completely white and cold. At first I thought he would almost certainly lose his leg, but we used to treat his leg with ice packs, cutting down to a minimum the rate of formation of harmful waste products in the tissues which could not be taken away by the blood vessels in spasm. After about twenty four hours the leg would slowly regain its colour as the spasm in the main arteries relaxed, and we could think about removing the shrapnel.*

*We got to know Sousse quite well, and we often used to visit the officers mess there. One evening when I was sitting in the bar there with Sid we received a call from the French medical officer who was in a highly excited state and wanted Sid to come over to see him at once. Sid had met him on one of our trips to the hospitals and had shown him round a few places at Sousse. We left at once wondering why the M.O. sounded so nervous. We arrived at his house and he said he would take us on in his car. Apparently one of the young girls had died in the French brothel and he was the medical officer in charge of all the girls' health. His car made its way round the back streets and drew up outside a building which I would have mistaken for a hotel. We went up the steps and through the front door where there was a large room where the girls would congregate and have a drink with their clients. A stoutly built lady dressed in black with a heavily upholstered frontage entered the room and said something in French to the medical officer. Sid and I followed her up the stairs into a small bedroom where there was a shape on the bed covered with a white sheet. The madame drew back the sheet showing a slender figure of a girl, her long black flair disheveled all over her face and her naked pale body showing many signs of bruises and grazes. Apparently the poor girl had died after she had had 123 clients and she must have been unconscious while she received the last few. The memory of her pathetic little body lying there haunted me for many years.*

*It is strange how some men seem to enjoy inflicting pain to their partner and can become very violent when they are sexually aroused. We had one man on the boat to whom I had to give heavy sedation for a week before he went home on leave because he was anxious he might harm his wife in a fit of sexual passion.*

*We spent a few weeks in Sousse as the battle casualties were less after the first offensive, and we were not needed so urgently in Sicily – and while we were there our ship was inspected to see what damage had been done by the abnormal strain the boat had been given in its new role. It was found that the welding of the davits had started being pulled up from the deck so we were told we might have to go to Tunis for repairs.*

July 23  2 a.m. Cool at last, with breeze coming through my porthole speeding for Sousse again, and to bed, having forcibly ejected Brown, Green and Dove from cabin, but not before they have drunk my only bottle of water! Wireless reports position of H.S. *Tisea* and H.S. *Julian* we passed a few miles out from Syracuse. Another ship being bombed. Sousse at 10 a.m. and waiting instructions to unload. 2 p.m. All patients disembarked and letters censored and taken ashore. Go for a bathe on beach about ½ mile away – amazing sight along the bombed and blasted harbour. T.S.L. being loaded with vehicles for Sicily. Ships full of barrels of oil being rolled down ramps by Arabs. Coal being passed along in little baskets by a chain of Arabs. All the houses in ruins, especially along the waterfront. Glaring white sand so hot one can't lie on it. Thousands of brown bodies in the sea, "new boys" unmistakable by the whiteness of their skins. Sea deep blue, and jade green. Tried to buy some melons, but seller would only take francs and I had English, Gibraltar, and Italian money only – currency an awful nuisance. Free issue of 50 cigarettes, piece of chocolate and box of matches today, but no sign of mail. In evening taken for a bathe by the E.M.O. in his jeep to a beach about 5 miles away – along dusty roads with military traffic roaring down the centre and Arabs and all races in the dust at the sides, riding bicycles, driving strange looking carts, riding donkeys. Found melons, cucumbers and pumpkin growing on the sand by the sea shore. The water was being drawn up from a well by means of a Heath Robinson apparatus pulled by a bored looking camel. Survey Officer came out to examine the water ambulances, so have a quiet day which we spend bathing. Thunderstorm and rain evening, and sea got up a bit. Fell getting on to ship from one of the water ambulances and cut my knee. Thought I had fractured my patella. Green wanted to excise the wound but I wasn't having any.

July 25   Stewart and I go ashore at 9 a.m. to 71st General Hospital to have our foot and patella respectively X-rayed. No broken bones. I also collect 45 pints of blood to take to Sicily, as we are sailing at noon. Part of 71st in original French hospital, rest in grounds. Tents on the dusty dry earth. We send all our most urgent cases to 71st, others, who can travel better, further

up country.
1.30 p.m. En route for Sicily once more. Grand to get a breeze through the ship again. Passed Pantelleria on the port beam about sundown, and missed a floating mine by about 100 yards – the second we have missed in 3 days! My knee very painful and oedematous.

July 26   Entered Syracuse harbour about 9 a.m. Heavy aerial attack overnight. Tanker in flames and belching out clouds of black smoke, just settling after being hit by 2 bombs. Another merchant ship also beginning to settle with a large gaping hole in her side – clouds of smoke rising from town. 8th Army reported to be regrouping and casualties are fewer in the last day or so. Men came out as usual to trade lemons and tomatoes. When our fellows shouted to them "Mussolini no good abdicato" they replied "Mussolini", spat into the sea then put a rope round their neck and pretended to hang themselves. Traded one bar of chocolate for four lemons. Loaded with 170 casualties including 51 Italian and Germans. 2 severe head cases. Casualty 1, Canadian, with fractured bone in parietal region – previously labelled as hysteria. X-ray showed missile which was removed. Casualty 2, German, temporal wound – loss of speech, left hemiplegia and right facial paralysis. Note that scalp cranium has been removed en bloc: result hernia cerebrium through duramater.
4 p.m. Away from Syracuse on route for Sousse. Stifling night. Went round the wards at 3 a.m. Heavy sea causing ship to roll and reducing both patients and night staff to sickness. Found night orderly in F ward asleep in cot – pretended he was a patient in the semi-dark, but had him on the mat. Still hotter at Sousse at 10 a.m. – wind feels as if it had come from the Sahara. Managed to get to beach to have a bathe after evacuating all the patients. Seems to have done my knee good, and I can walk a bit better.

Stung by a jelly fish on the chest while bathing, has caused an urticarial eruption. Officer from 71st Hospital came on board. He had landed at Pantellaria and said everyone was very friendly. One L.C.I. officer and 80 men of the guards accompanied by one destroyer and escort vessel went on to Lampedusa and ordered the surrender of the garrison of 4,500. They had not enough men to disarm the Italians so the Italian officers offered to disarm their own men. Heard story of one district where complaints were made that men's letters were going astray. Investigations at the Army P.O. proved that the Sorting Clerk could not read or write! (He must have been sorting our mail.)

July 28   Went up with Green to see Field Surgical Unit. Drove in lorry which carried the Frigidaire for blood transfusion unit. Appalling road – inches of dust – chiefly cactus and olive groves with some large aloe plant. Major Geoffrey Parker in charge of F.S.U. found he was at Crookham with me. O.C. Surgical Div. of Hospital (Col. d'Abreu) was in mess – lectured to us at Crookham. He considered that F.S.U. were impracticable in modern war, as however good a surgeon may be he is unable numerically to deal with the cases. He considered that the C.C.S. should be the ideal place for initial operations. Found Hodson was radiologist at hospital who was at Crookham with me. We used to play bridge there. Car drove us back to Sousse. Had a bathe on beach – although we had no togs or towels, dried in sun in five minutes. Stung by another jelly fish – worse than last night. Medusa-like creature with long hairs which stick on to one's skin – large weals all over my arm. Sabotage of the water pipeline has reduced water supply to almost nil – we have been unable to refill our tanks.

July 30   Along quayside refilling with water – but still no oil so we are unable to move. *Julian* left for Sicily midday yesterday.

Shark round ship yesterday drove the bathers to the one rope ladder up the ship's side like ducks with a fox after then.

August 2   Bank Holiday – and a lovely day for it. Baking sun, hot wind blowing into your eyes, ears, mouth, so every time you close your teeth they grate and crunch the dust. A tanker appeared last night with a destroyer escort so perhaps we get some oil and leave this dust-ridden spot. Melons and bathing are the best points about it.

August 4   29 years since the last war began on August 4th 1914. Went alongside tanker this morning and oiled. Tried to have a bathe, but sea covered with oil. Went on to beach this afternoon, sweltering, only relieved by getting into sea. This evening had a few spots of rain – everyone collected forward of the bridge to feel it on their bodies. Soon stopped, and we are back to where we were with sweat streaming down – most of us have a towel to keep mopping. *David* returned from Sicily this morning. British 8th Army, 78th, 50th and 51st divisions with Canadian on left flank and Yanks along N coast now attacking the slopes of Mount Etna.

August 5   Grand news tonight that we have taken Catania. 6.30 p.m. Orders to sail for Tunis. Thank heaven we are leaving this sweltering cesspool. We sail due east at first and follow a complicated course through a recently swept lane through the mines.

August 7 Tied up in Tunis harbor to a bombed and partially sunk Italian ship. Tunis is about 5 miles from the sea, and we sail down a canal in the midst of the Tunis Lake. As usual harbour littered with sunken and bombed ships. All the buildings round the harbour are blasted to rubble, but the main town of Tunis is in good order. Full of Americans, British, French, both soldiers and girls, Arabs, Negroes. Went on a lorry to 97 General Hospital hoping to see George Ormiston but he was away. Ten miles through dried, burnt up country, with dusty vines, cactus and aloes. Remnants of smashed up German guns and lorries, old gun positions and trenches. Military traffic roaring down a small tarmac strip full of potholes in the centre of the road, while Arabs riding donkeys or driving skinny ponies occupy the dust on either side. Passed a dried up lake outside Tunis – its bottom smooth as a pancake and covered with salt. Dysentery and malaria rife and the 97 Hospital rampant with it. This harbour stinks of sewage and we are covered with flies all day and mosquitoes all night.

August 8   Sunday, had a lift in a car to Hamman Liff, where Von Arnhem was captured – battered German planes, guns, lorries even an old tank stuck in the sea. Shell holes and rubble. Strong wind blew sand into nose, throat, mouth and ears, made one filthy. Just heard that the A.D.H., who has been making himself most unpopular by insisting that all men who get malaria and dysentery do so by not following his instruction and should be punished, has been admitted to hospital with both malaria and dysentery. Even the A.D.M.S. has not yet stopped laughing. A.D.M. told us he wrote to his wife and told her that he was being very faithful to her and in any case he would never look at any women under 50 – as they never yell, they never tell, they never swell and always say thank you! Repairs progressing. French workmen working on one side of ship, R.E.s the other. All ranks taking Mepachrine against malaria.

August 10   Stayed night 97th General Hospital with George Ormiston. Went in truck with Green and 12 orderlies who are going on temporary duty. Found George under a shower and joined him. Plenty of water but very little booze. Went round hospital with him at night – 1,200 beds. Slept under canvas open at the end, awoke 3 a.m. with my mouth full of dust. Came back with ophthalmic specialist into Tunis. Arrived just as the welding plant motor weighing some tons fell into harbour. Diver now trying to locate its position, and work on ship held up.

*We were at Tunis much longer than expected because when the heavy welding plant weighing several tons was being brought out to the Dinard to carry out our repairs it fell overboard into the bottom of the harbour – it was about ten days before divers located it and it was hauled up. I was quite pleased to have the opportunity of exploring the area, particularly as Carthage was quite close. During my school days at Greshams during Latin and Greek it was only a name, now there was an opportunity to visit the ruined city. It was a great thrill for me to imagine the way of life which the crumbled walls and pillars must have supported so many years ago. Somehow I felt it helped me to think more objectively about the present predicament we were in. This was nothing new this war of ours – it is a strange weakness of human beings and for as long as our knowledge of civilisation stretches human beings have behaved as we were behaving – so I was taking part in probably one page, or even one paragraph, of a continuous pageant.*

*We used to visit the 97th General Hospital at Tunis fairly frequently and made a lot of friends in the mess.*

August 11   Lorry-hopped out to 97 General again last night and had a good evening in the mess. Grand walk after dinner in bright moonlight over the country. Tracks of tanks from the chase of the Boche by the 1st Army can still be seen, and numerous casualties have resulted from the unwary setting off undetected mines. Did some work on malaria this morning, and have familiarised myself with the technique. We have all bought fly swatters and hope to get some peace. Bought Dickie some more soldiers and a gay basket for O. I am very popular with the D.C.97 General as I took him a bottle of sherry and George ½ bottle of gin – no more booze for me this week.

August 12   Made an early start armed with sandwiches and bottle of beer, was picked up by a Yank in a jeep en route for Carthage. Straight down to sea N of Tunis. Boiling hot sun, was glad of my topee. Passed the Tunis Airport of El Arouin – masses of our planes lined up, nearby hundreds of derelict German and Italian planes, the ground looking like patchwork from the repairs done after our RAF strafed the landing grounds. Went over the ruins of Roman Carthage (Romans destroyed original Carthage in 145 B.C.). Walked round the amphitheatre where Churchill addressed the troops. Down to the beach to eat my sandwiches and bathe in deep blue sea. Back to ship by 4.30. George Ormiston came to dinner, and I went back with him to make early start as I was detailed for charge of evacuation of wounded to Philippeville by air.

*We had several serious casualty cases which we were told were to be evacuated to Philippeville by air – as the hospital there had better facilities. Sid Green was anxious to go on the trip to relieve the boredom of waiting for our repairs to be completed so insisted there should be a medical officer on each plane, himself in one and his General Duties Officer in the other – Capt. Squires.*

*We were not so excited about the trip when one of the American pilots said that on the run the previous week the tail of his aeroplane had been shot off by American fighters who mistook him for a German plane and only just managed to land his crippled plane.*

August 13   Left 97 General with ambulances for air evacuation at 7 a.m. Loaded 11 stretchers into large Douglas troop transport plane, manned by Yanks. Twenty plane loads in all from El

Arouin airport. Glad to say we made an uneventful journey. Flying about 5,000 ft the earth looked all colours of yellow, brown and gold flanked by the very blue sea – Bizerta, Bone, eventually Philippeville by 11 a.m. Directly we landed pilot and co-pilot made a rush from the plane. I thought they were making for cover but they returned in a few minutes with a sack of grapes pinched from the neighbouring vineyards. Then the ambulances arrived and we unloaded the cases and dispatched them to 67 Hospital. Into the plane again, and made for Tunis. Pilot and co-pilot sitting in front holding joy stick and shoving grapes into their mouths. Radio officer and another member of crew pulled out stretchers, slept till Tunis. I sat in the tail which was rather lively. Reached Tunis 1 p.m. having completed 500 miles.

*We often used to go to the R.A.F. station at Hammamet. Of course we were very popular because of our contact with the 97th General Hospital and their nursing staff and so we had an open invitation to visit them whenever we liked as long as we brought along as many of the nurses as possible*

August 14   Went to party with RAF at Hammamet at 7 p.m. Four Medical Officers and some Sisters from 97 General. Drove 52 miles across the Bon Peninsula to aerodrome along the sea shore. A most romantic setting. The mess tent was decorated with an "olde English" bar made out of red and blue paper and trestles at the far end, lit with coloured lamps. Little tables had all sorts of things to eat, and whisky and beer ad lib. A canvas pathway led to the dance floor between the tent and the sea. RAF band, and we danced on canvas laid on the sand. A full moon lit up beach and the sea. How they managed to make so much out of so little I don't know. Quite pathetic the excitement that came into their very youthful faces when they saw the Sisters arriving. I lay off, and only danced once with a grey haired sister with the result I drank too much and spent most of evening hunting in Ireland with a fellow whose wife had gone into joint mastership of the Meath Hunt. At 2 a.m. we all went into the sea and had a bathe in the moonlight. Back to the ship by 5 a.m. as dawn was breaking. Glad to say I was still able to climb the rope ladder up the ship's side.

August 15   Green and I set out after lunch for Carthage and were picked up by two Yankee officers in a big car. Both in the Air Force – one of them had been over Rome on Friday (when I was in the plane going to Philippeville, 84 Fortresses passed over our head). Took us back to their mess to drink brandy and lemonade and brandy and Benedictine. Then to La Marsa, a fascinating village by the sea shore, hoping for dinner, but no luck, so they drove back to Tunis to eat melon, tunny fish, avocado pear, grilled liver, grilled steak, fried potatoes and spaghetti, peaches, nectarines, grapes and a bottle of wine. Seldom felt so full in all my life.

*Eventually our repairs were completed and we were back into the same routine – taking casualties off Sicily.*

August 17   10.30 a.m. Sailed from Tunis for Bizerta. Saw flock of flamingoes on Tunis Lake as we left; they took flight like a pink cloud when we blew our whistle. 5 p.m. Oiling from a tanker in Bizerta harbour. Had a good bathe while the portside barges were in the water. Harbour and outside crowded with ships. 9 p.m. Just as we left the tanker in the inner harbour enemy planes appeared overhead, dropped flares that lighted up every ship – terrific barrage of pompoms "Chicago piano" and heavy AA from warships. Bombs of every calibre dropped. One hit tanker, and blazing oil outshone the flares. We were meanwhile manoeuvring to get out of the narrow harbour which was blocked by a sunken ship. Missed a cruiser by a few feet – failed to pick up two of our barges in the confusion. They followed us out, but the motor of one failed and was unable to make the ship. Towed by an M.L. we eventually hitched it on the davits, and hoisted it, meanwhile the crumps of bomb, AA shells, exploding over our heads, and rattles of falling shrapnel on the deck sounded like a continuous gigantic thunder and hailstorm. Had the satisfaction of seeing one plane caught in the searchlights and shot down blazing into the sea. Meanwhile we were starting on our way, having been ordered to report at Catania by 5 p.m. tomorrow. Our troubles were not over, however, as a plane dropped flares on us and followed us to sea and dropped a stick of bombs on the starboard beam, circled and dropped two more over the port bow. Think it must have run out of bombs by that time, as we were left in peace with no damage, heading for Sicily at 18 knots leaving Bizerta blazing behind.

August 18  11 a.m. Malta a few miles off to starboard. Shipping between Malta and Sicily being bombed continuously, and looks as if we are running into a lively show. Arrived Catania about 5 p.m. all quiet – ambulances waiting for us on the battered quayside, greater part of damage done by the Jerries before they left. More modern looking town than Syracuse. Left 9 p.m.

*Later that month after we had unloaded our casualties at the N. African port at Bone we had orders to proceed at once into the Messina Straits as the allies were landing in Italy.*

August 19  11 a.m. Running along at 13 knots quite close to Pantelleria, rugged looking island on the port beam. Busy morning with plenty of interesting work. Not much surgical work, but plenty of malaria – glad I went to 97th Hospital, as I have about 30 slides to stain and examine this afternoon. 5 p.m.

Found rubber dinghy floating in sea soon after passing Cape Bon, circled round but no trace of airman. RAF rescue launch appeared and we left the search to them. Emergency operation 8 p.m. on fellow who had a Very light shot through palm – fracture carpal bone – wad picked up in extensor tendons. Finished staining and examining slides by 12.30 and to bed.

August 20  5 a.m. Passed convoy travelling east with minesweepers and destroyers. 7 a.m. Running into Philippeville looking marvellous in morning light. Not so parched and burnt as the places we have been to. Closer to, looks like a small edition of Torquay quayside covered by troops (Seaforths and Black Watch) awaiting embarkation, wire netting and ramps. No sign of damage to the port – quite refreshing to see. Troops embarking all morning on the Laetitia (which was with us at Gourock on the Clyde) and which was escorted out by three destroyers in the afternoon. Marvellous bathe in the afternoon, from a sandy bay with good diving rocks, water deep blue and clear. In the evening went with Sid and two Sisters to drink vin blanc at the Officers Club and had another dinner at the Littoria with vin rosé. All felt pretty good, so went down for a bathe in the moonlight and back to ship at 1 a.m. Received oil from a destroyer.

August 21  Left Philippeville at 8 a.m., calm as a duck pond. Felt quite sad we were not staying longer, as it was such a lovely place, really more like the South of France than N. Africa. Arrived Bone at midday, and went straight into harbour for more oil and water. Very busy harbour with plenty of shipping. Had a good bathe, and did some shopping. Saw ship carrying 1,800 prisoners of war torpedoed by aerial torpedo. Hole blown in side 50 by 20 feet. 400 prisoners killed, and bodies being washed up continuously. Ship beached at St Cloud a mile away. Last night the hottest we've had, wedged in harbour alongside an American freighter. Not a breath of air, dripping with sweat, mattress saturated.

August 23   In disgrace – nearly missed the ship last night through unexpected orders to sail for Syracuse. Sid and I were out at the Officers Club with two Sisters, two Sappers and a naval bloke having a party. Arrived back at 12.45 and told the ship had sailed. Luckily a plank was laid from a Yankee ship to the *Dinard* which had just lifted the hawsers, and Sid, I and the two Sisters just made it. Hell to pay. French pilot in hysterics of rage. Captain telling us off like schoolboys, O.C. pathetically telling us we would never live it down. The matron giving tongue because the sisters had orders to be in cabins by 11.30. Glad to say this morning by eating humble pie things are looking a little brighter.

August 24   Arrived Syracuse about 8 a.m. Went alongside quay to load about 250 cases including about 70 prisoners of war. Large number of medical cases – busy staining and examining malarial slides. Left Syracuse at 2 p.m. for Philippeville.

August 25   Busy day – one German with cerebral malaria with tetany, looks as if he will pass out. Another, Italian, with fractured pelvis, torn urethra, fractured femur has been in an Italian hospital in Sicily for two months. No effort been made to reduce pelvis or femur – only young boy.

August 26   Berthed at Philippeville at 07.30, all cases evacuated by 10 a.m. Afraid we shall not stop long, as we are down to 15 tons of oil, and we cannot get any here. Sailed for Bone midday.

August 27   Out to the 5th General with the C.O. to do some more malarial work, especially their special technique of staining a thick drop with methylene blue and eoisin in one minute. Parasites showing up isolated, with the R.B.Cs haemolysed.

September 1   Received a signal from Naval Station to send for our mail. Great excitement when four sacks were brought on board – opening them we found a few parcels, but chiefly washing belonging to the recently attached RAMC personnel. Not a letter. Work on the engines now completed, damage done by the concussion of the "near misses" at Bizerta was more serious than was thought and put the starboard engine out of action.

September 2   Sailed from Bone, 2 p.m., with orders to report at St Augusta with all speed – just time to fill to capacity with oil but no time for water. Deep blue sea with fresh breeze and quite a swell.

September 3   Invasion of Italy across Messina Straits by British and Canadian troops at 4.30 a.m., preceded by aerial and naval bombardment. 4 p.m. Off Cape Pessaro. Passed part of the battle fleet steaming S. Six destroyers with two battleships of Queen Elizabeth class.

# Chapter 12

# Italy and Yugoslavia

The next day (September 4) I put up my third pip, marking my promotion to Captain, RAMC. We were ordered to Santa Theresa in the straits of Messina, and anchored for the night just south of the operational area. But there were practically no casualties for us, and we moved on south to Catania. From there we went back to Philippeville. That was an unpleasant passage. There was a stiff westerly wind, putting up a heavy sea, and we ran into a heavy air-raid off Bizerta. There was a brilliant moon, and a multitude of flares showed up our ships as planes dived to deliver bombs. It was a very rough and unpleasant hour.

On September 8 the surrender of Italy was announced, and we had a grand celebration in my cabin. It was just as well that we had something to drink, as fuel oil had contaminated our water. The collapse of Italy no doubt justified a celebration but the bitterest fighting of the Italian campaign was still to come, as the Germans tenaciously resisted our advance. Early in the morning of September 14 I had my own first landing on Italian soil. It was at the tiny harbour of Pizzo, into which we had to go stern first to pick up casualties. The Germans were holding the high ground commanding the beaches, and were sending mortar shells into the village. We walked through the village street and came to a house that had just been occupied by the Commandos. They had put a notice on the door saying "Do not Disturb".

General Montgomery was in the village, arranging to create a diversion around Salerno. We loaded about 170 casualties, called at Reggio in the afternoon for some more, and went on to Catania, where we found the boom closed, and had to anchor outside for the night. The organisation by the hospital ships was not good – there seemed next to no coordination between the various ports. Although the people at Pizzo had promised to send a signal to Reggio giving the time of our arrival and the number of casualties we could take, nobody at Reggio seemed to know that we were coming. At Catania we were ordered back to Philippeville, but when we were about 100 milles from Philippeville we got a signal saying that the hospital there was full, and ordering us to Tripoli instead. "A proper lash up," remarked my corporal.

We unloaded our casualties at Tripoli, and were then sent to Salerno. We found the gulf packed with ships, and a destroyer signalled to us that the port was closed. Then there was a heavy air-raid, and the destroyers tried to envelop us with smoke. Shipping was also being shelled by German batteries on shore, and some of the shells landed unpleasantly close.

We hung on at Salerno for three days, until all the wards were full of wounded men, some, alas, without much chance of survival. There were many cases of what we used to call "shell shock", now termed "anxiety state", some with gross tremors, and in a semi-stuporous state. One boy, a Marine, had been hit in the arm, causing a fracture of the humerus. In a German counter-attack his unit had to fall back, but he was unable to make it, owing to shock and loss of blood. He was found by some German stretcher bearers, who dressed his wounds, gave him a cigarette, and told him to fend for himself. He crawled into a village, where the priest took him into his house, put him to bed and nursed him. He was there from September 10-23, when the Allied troops took the village and he was found and sent to us.

We spent the rest of 1943 on what had become our regular routine, collecting casualties from Italy, and taking them to base hospitals in North Africa. Some of our passages were very rough. There was one appalling night when the ship so pitched and rolled that there were times when we doubted if she could ever right herself again. All the double-tier cots in one ward collapsed, and the patients in them were flung to the deck. Water poured into the dispensary, and I spent most of the night trying to rescue floating cylinders of oxygen, and to save our precious supplies of drugs. We could still manage an occasional laugh, though. At breakfast next morning one of the Sisters said that her chest kept coming forward, and could one of the men screw it down for her? Another Sister said that her drawers kept coming open all night – even the Matron smiled.

At the end of September we were still running to Salerno but it was much quieter than on our earlier trips. The Germans had been pushed back from the hills that overlook the town, and we were able to go right in to load the casualties who had been brought down from the front.

Malaria was rampant among our troops, and some of them were very ill with it. Every minute that could be spared from urgent surgery was spent in examining malarial slides. At the beginning of October we took a large number of malarial cases to hospital at Tripoli, and we had a few days in port there. We had some pleasant bathing, but food was short, and the only place where we could get a meal was at the YMCA. Glasses were practically non-existent, but some ingenious chap had thought of cutting bottles in two, and using the bottom halves for glasses. They served well.

Mid-October found us in Naples, where we evacuated 224 wounded men, mostly surgical cases from the 5th Army. One lad, a Yorkshireman had a huge wound in his thigh – it must have been made by a spinning rifle bullet at close range. While

I was dressing it he said, in broad Yorkshire, "Ah could put oop with this packet if they had brought poor Mother oop from river." Seeing me completely mystified, he explained "Ah were holding bridgehead wi' twenty others when Jerry cooms and drops mortars on us. Then they blows oop bridge, like, and blows us in river. Our blokes cooms and fetches I oop like, but poor Mother was left on bottom, like." Having expressed sympathy for his mother, I discovered that it was his wallet with his mother's photograph in it that had not been retrieved.

Later in October we had a break in our routine by being ordered to take a number of cases to Malta. We were in illustrious company in the Grand Harbour – the battleships *Rodney* and *Nelson* were there, and the *Warspite* was being repaired after her hammering at Salerno. Valetta showed signs of heavier damage than any other place I had seen: hundred of houses had been reduced to rubble, and the harbour was littered with sunken ships, only the tops of their masts showing above water, and with great cranes working feverishly to recover vital parts from the wreckage. A friend (Briggs) from my St Thomas's days was commanding a field ambulance in Malta, and it was nice to get in touch with him. We had some very expensive drinks together in a bar in what was left of the town.

From Malta we went back to Naples, and as we were not needed for a couple of days we were able to do some sightseeing. Pompeii was marvellous, even after the 178 bombs which were said to have fallen on it. We went through a vicious air-raid while we were at anchor off Naples. We were just finishing dinner when a huge explosion spilt our coffee, and made the old ship shiver in every timber. Then every ship in Naples opened up with a terrific barrage. The German attack lasted for about 40 minutes, and we were repeatedly dive-bombed, the planes coming in so close that it seemed as though they would land on deck. We felt that the end really had come for old *Dinard* of Dunkirk, but somehow she came through the bombardment none the worse.

At the beginning of November we were sent to Taranto to pick up 216 cases. The place was looking quite civilised, with trains running. A restaurant had been turned into a splendid Officers' Club. There was a band, and plenty of Vermouth to drink – but, alas, nothing to put in it. One officer there told me about a landing he had made. His landing craft ran up the beach, down went the gangway, and he rushed forward, waving his revolver and exhorting his men to follow him in the face of whatever they might meet. They charged up the beach, with rifles, tommy guns and hand grenades at the ready, and rounded a corner into the village street. There they were halted suddenly – by a little Italian girl with a basket of lemons, which she was offering for sale!

As the fighting in Italy extended, so did our itinerary, and we were soon making frequent trips to Brindisi and Bari on the Adriatic. We were much troubled by mines, laid by low-flying aircraft. On our first trip to Bari (November 17, 1943) we were signalled to stop outside the harbour because of mines. A destroyer was blown up near the entrance to the port, and the naval authorities were afraid to allow us to take casualties on board. After hanging about for two days we were ordered back to Brindisi, and the casualties were sent there from Bari by road.

I went ashore, and found Brindisi an attractive old town. An Officers' Club had just been opened in a house that had been a German Officers' Club. The swastika had been painted over with red, white and blue.

We embarked 198 cases, and took them to Malta; we collected my friend Briggs and his Field Ambulance to transport them to Brindisi. They were a cheerful lot and nice to have on board, but they made rather a hole in the gin ration.

We were held up at Brindisi for a week, unable to go on to Bari because of mines. Casualties were sent back to Taranto by air, and we went there to pick them up. We took on 229 cases, mostly severely injured battle casualties, and sailed with them for the base hospital at Philippeville. Everyone there was pleased to see us, for it had been reported that we had gone down after hitting a mine in the Adriatic.

On December 8 at Philippeville we got ten bags of mail, including 8 letters for me from O. written at various dates between July and November. Tempers on board, which had been getting a bit short, were transformed by the arrival of our mail, and all was peace and goodwill. Another notable event at Philippeville was that we were able to collect our Christmas drink ration from the NAAFI, providing two bottles of beer for every man.

On December 11 we sailed for Sicily. We fuelled and watered at Augusta, and were then ordered once more to Bari. This time we were able to enter harbour; it was a scene of utter devastation, with burned and blown-up ships everywhere. At Bari we were given orders to proceed 120 miles north to Termoli, to embark casualties from the beach. That was an appalling trip. We had to sail by night and there were no lights anywhere. Inshore was a rocky coast, and outside a narrow, swept path the sea was a maze of minefields. By the grace of God we hit nothing, and anchored off Termoli by about 07.00.

The sea there is shallow, and we had to stay about half a mile offshore. We sent off our specially equipped boats – "sea ambulances" for the wounded men and they had a difficult time in the shallow, choppy water. They had to run their bows on the beach and put out kedge anchors to hold their sterns while the casualties were loaded. Getting back on board was no easier for the choppy sea made it hard to fix the slings from the davits, and as the boats came up they were liable to be swung against the ship's side, making things difficult and dangerous for the wounded. However, we had all the wounded on board by early afternoon. Then for some reason, the naval authorities would not let us leave until 5 p.m., which meant another hair-raising night passage. But we had little time to think about the dangers outside, for we were busy all night in the operating theatre, doing what we could for the worst cases.

We were then sent to Algiers, where we arrived in the early evening of Christmas Day. We were unable to get in touch with anyone inside, so we could not enter harbour, and had to anchor off for the night. It was a horrible night, with a heavy swell running. We rolled and pitched all night, which was a great tax on the severely wounded men, and no one got a wink of sleep. On top of this we had to keep steam on the main engines for fear of dragging, and we were running short of fuel.

On Boxing Day we made a signal to the authorities saying that we were almost out of fuel, and asking for tugs to be sent out to help us to keep station. That stirred up some action and we were allowed to enter harbour. There was plenty of room, and we could easily have come in the night before. The patient in my ward had an arterial haemorrhage brought on by the appalling buffeting, and I insisted that he should be evacuated to the general hospital forthwith. That required a great deal of "pushing", and we all felt thoroughly disgruntled. We had brought our wounded some 1,100 miles from the beaches, only to be treated as if we were just a nuisance.

We had our delayed Christmas dinner in port on December 29 and sailed next day on what should have been a pleasant trip – taking 66 Sisters and Red Cross girls to Naples, Alas, it turned out to be anything but pleasant. My diary for December 31, 1943 – Jan 1, 1944 tells the story:

Last night we raised an impromptu concert for everyone, and tonight I was going to get up a dance in C ward – with 66 sisters and Red Cross girls we could have had a good time. But at 5.30 a.m. this morning the wind began rising, the sea got up, and being on the beam we are getting the full force of it. At breakfast things began to get lively and all the breakfast things collapsed on to the floor. Hot coffee and milk which had been put on the sideboard flew off when the marble top became detached. The scalding milk went down a Sister's back, and she had to be rushed to her cabin to remove her clothes. The wind rose from gale to hurricane force and at 2.30 p.m. the ship, catching a heavy broadside, collapsed on her side. The lashings of 1 and 3 starboard boats became adrift, and all hands were summoned to the boat deck. A lifeline was made taut down the side of the deck, and we all helped to make the boats fast – a most precarious and difficult job, with seas being shipped continuously, and the hurricane shrieking through the rigging. Our course was then altered to meet the sea head on, and with the engines at half speed we just managed to stay and maintain this position. Scenes of complete devastation everywhere, floors covered with vomit and sea water, the well deck flooded, and all the cabins and wards leaking sea water on to the unfortunate sisters and Red Cross, most of whom were completely flattened out. No food could be cooked, and we lived on cups of tea and bread and Spam. Another mountainous sea struck the ship broadside, and smashed the davit and No. 2 boat. The boat was left dangling on one davit, and there was nothing for it but to try to cut the hawser. This was done, and our beautiful sea ambulance with its valuable 60 h.p. engine disappeared into the sea.

I stayed up to see the New Year in, and prayed that the New Year would still the wind and the sea. My bed being sopping, and the floor and settee covered with water, I just wrapped a greatcoat round me and lay on the bed. Sleep was impossible with the ship standing on her head, lying on her side and enveloped in thunderous breaking seas and surf.

This morning (New Year's Day) I was glad to have a cup of tea, hoped that the weather was abating. But the sea is rising more than ever. We are living in hopes that things will improve before we run out of oil. That fact, and also that we are off our course and the sea infested with our own mines as well as Jerry's, makes the prospect somewhat grim. Alec and I inspected the remaining 5 sea ambulances – there was not one which is sound. Some are stove in, the tops of the engines have come off, and the engines are being soused with salt water. Some of the compasses have been broken off and washed overboard. We are reduced to two lifeboats and an odd raft or so for over 200 people.

There has not been a sign of another ship for 36 hours. We have had S.O.S. calls from others, but we are unable to answer or help them. After the storm had been on for 12 hours we received an Admiralty warning to all ships to return to port. This we cannot do. To turn and make for N. Africa and risk a broadside from the sea, the captain says, would be the end of the *Dinard*. So on we go, with our only hope to ride out the storm before our oil runs out.

That evening the storm abated somewhat, and the Captain decided to try to turn the ship and run for Bone, which was about 100 miles away. Gradually he eased her round, and after a tricky hour or so we were running before the storm.

We made Bone safely next day, and when lipstick appeared among our nurses and Red Cross girls we felt that things were better. But what a sight the poor old *Dinard* looked There was not a dry bed on the ship, and wet clothes, bedding and pillows were scattered everywhere. The damage on deck was astounding – one 4 inch solid steel davit snapped off, and massive steel rails twisted like corkscrews. Still, the lipstick had reappeared. Next day I got up a dance and we forgot our troubles.

We lost our trip to Naples because we could not go to sea without repairs. The nurses and Red Cross girls were transferred to another ship, and we all stayed in Bone for nearly a fortnight.

Then we were sent to Taranto, to embark wounded partisans who had been brought there from Yugoslavia.

These extracts from my diary illustrate the stark aspects of this war.

January 15, 1944 (Taranto). Embarked 227 cases, all Yugoslavs. The most ghastly lot of wounds we have had – some wounded months ago have lain hidden in the mountains without any sort of medical attention. All the wounds suppurating, grenade wounds of the face with the skin peppered with fragments, eyes disorganised. In M ward I have boys of 13, 14, 16 – the little boy of 14 dressed in tattered remnants of the uniforms of all nationalitiës was captured by the Jerries. Being a guerrilla he knew what his fate would be. He was rescued just in time, but he had lost his voice – the fright was too great even for his gallant heart. He is very seasick today, which adds to his unhappiness. A ward is full of girls, all chattering like parrots. Some are only 15, with their hair plaited like heron's mane. Some are severely wounded, and cannot rise. Those who can, walk out into the men's wards at every opportunity, scandalising the Matron. Were it not for the Red Cross pyjamas they would go out in their bandages alone. It means nothing to them – they have lived and fought beside the men for months. They shriek with laughter when they are hustled back. Here and there is a man who can talk French and we have to put our questions to him, and he interprets the answer of Yugoslavs.

Never have we carried such a ship full of tragedy and never have I seen such sorrows hidden by such gay and dauntless hearts.

We took our Yugoslavs to hospital in Malta, and at once went back to Taranto for more.

January 22. (Taranto). Embarked 220 Yugoslavs – again a ghastly cargo of mangled humanity, made worse by the lack of early treatment. Also about 50 cases of pulmonary TB. The young fighting girls and boys are mixed up together and it is not easy to say what their sex is. One youngster with short hair and battledress, speaking only Yugoslav, was quite a problem. I said 'A girl', the staff nurse said 'A boy', the Sgt. Major said 'A boy', the E.M.O. said 'Definitely boy'. An interpreter had to be produced to clinch the diagnosis by word of mouth rather than anatomical facts!

There were many peripheral nerve injuries, radial, ulnar and median palsies, some combined where a bullet had shattered the axillary portion of the humerus, producing a complete paralysis. A student who spoke English said that the Germans were holding the towns in Yugoslavia and made sorties into the country districts for food, robbing the peasants without any attempt at payment. The partisans hid in the mountains, and descended on the German units, ambushing and massacring them. When reinforcements arrived the Partisans disappeared. The night our patient left, two brigades of Partisans engaged the Jerries in a tip and run battle. All the casualties, meanwhile, were brought down on mules and carts to the coast, where our light torpedo craft and Yugoslav schooners were waiting, and they were all embarked. When all was clear, the Partisans slipped away by tracks known only to themselves, and by morning the Jerries found they were fighting nobody.

After disembarking our second complement of Yugoslavs in Malta, we were sent to Naples, to take part – though naturally we were not given advance information at the time – in the Anzio landings. Again, I think, some extracts from my diary, rough as they are, may give some idea of that horrible period.

January 24. 6 p.m. Arrived Naples, to be greeted immediately by an air-raid warning. At anchor blacked out, lying outside the harbour, being enveloped in most suffocating smokescreen.

8 p.m. News received *Leinster* bombed and hit – *Andrew* bombed – *David* sunk (all these were hospital ships). *Andrew* picking up survivors. Great air of depression about the ship. We had many friends on the *David* and we fear that with this heavy sea that is running the rescue operation will be difficult. We are lying here with very little oil, and cannot move far.

January 25. A disturbed night with little sleep – depth charges going off every few minutes, air-raid warnings and sound of aircraft, continuous smokescreen enveloping all the shipping. Moved into the Bay of Naples with *Leinster* and *Andrew*. Latter two gone into the harbour. No definite news as yet - cruisers, destroyers, submarines, patrol craft, troopers, tankers all round us. Rough sea would still make operations difficult with our ambulance craft.
9 p.m. Moving into the inner harbour for oil, a most difficult and precarious job in the pitch black night. Harbour full of ships all completely blacked out. Now trying to get alongside a tanker. Orders to be upon the beaches at Nettuno by 11 a.m. tomorrow, travelling up alone without lights. A pleasant prospect before us: of the three hospital ships that went yesterday one is sunk, and the other two damaged and back in Naples. Perhaps fourth time lucky! Now to add to it all there is an air-raid going on over the harbour. What a picnic – trying to tie up to a tanker of all things, with this inferno going on. Being orderly officer just posted P.A.D. squad. To add to it all, as we were pulling up the anchor, leaving harbour about midnight, it fouled a buoy. Deuce of a job – luckily we had an Admiralty tug with us to prevent collision with other ships, and a man had to be let down over the side to hack it away.

January 26. Misfortune never comes alone, and here we are battling against a hell of a gale, with heavy seas beating over the foc'sle bridge and boat deck. Even with my ports all tightly shut water has poured on to my bed, and there is water on the floor. No cooking can be done, and we have had a few sandwiches. The trouble is that our rendezvous was for 11.30, and at 2 p.m. we're still about 100 miles off.

9 p.m. Still battling, and not able to make our objective until the gale abates. Flashes of gunfire and AA fire on the coast. The captain has turned the ship and now we have the sea on our stern. The ship is bit quieter this way, but we shall have to turn again or we shall be too far away by daybreak. Everybody finding life a bit trying.

January 27. (Anzio). 10 a.m. A sunny morning, sea abating, wind dropping, everyone's spirits rising. Running into the coast with large convoy of L.S.T.s, with destroyers, and corvette support. Anchor in bay outside Anzio. L.S.T.s being unloaded along beach, minesweepers clearing the sea, cruisers and destroyers watching the coast. Cruisers bombarding inland – the sea alive with craft of every description. Amphibians swimming ashore look like rats leaving a ship. No sooner had we dropped the hook than the red flag went up on every ship – "Air-raid imminent", followed by hum of aircraft overhead very high. Every warship loosing off, while other small craft lay smoke. Things lively with the barrage, whistling bombs falling in the sea (luckily so far in the sea). Plane shot down. Half hour, and another raid, plane shot down, saw pilot bale out, S.O.S. received from several ships for medical assistance for casualties – Sid Green went out in one ambulance boat, and I went in another. Collecting cases and bringing them on board. A choppy sea made it a bit difficult. All casualties had to be let down over the side in Neil-Robertson stretchers on to our ambulance boats, which were up here one moment, and twenty feet lower the next. Very difficult to prevent the patients swinging round and bashing their foreheads on the side of the ship. Another air-raid while we were in the middle of this – a pretty hot spot! Spitfires constantly patrolling overhead, but they don't seem to stop the Jerries coming over. Having collected our cases on the *Dinard* the ship was ordered to return to Naples.

Operating with Sid from 4 p.m. to 3 a.m. To bed by 3.30 a.m. A somewhat hectic three days, but running into Naples this morning. It feels like home.

January 28. Heard more details of the *David*. In company with the *Leinster* and *Andrew* about 30 miles off shore, they were attacked by aircraft for an hour. Dropping flares, the ships had no chance of evasion. Bomb dropped in the well deck of the *David*. Ship sank in 5 minutes, no chance to lower boats. The other 2 ships did not see her go down, but spotted the red lights on the life jackets, and a man signalling on a raft with a hand torch. They both turned, and with great difficulty launched some boats. Picked up all but 55 who are missing. Great strafe going on here about the lack of organisation of our hospital ships – no greater proof is needed than the way we have been treated this week.

January 29. 10 p.m. Ordered to sea to be off the beaches by daybreak. The captain spent the morning trying to obtain oil, and definitely told Naval Control that we could not sail without. He was treated like a bit of dirt. We had all day doing nothing, now they want to start this racket of oiling in the dark. Thick fog makes it impossible to move through this mass of supply ships, cruisers, destroyers, etc. to the tanker. The naval signalling station will not reply. The captain rightly refuses to move the ship.

January 30. Trying to get alongside the tanker, but the cruiser *Orion* has nipped in ahead of us. HMS *Mauritius* nearby. A Dido class cruiser, can't see her name, with the ensign at half mast, and shapes wrapped in Union Jacks on her stern, is going out to sea to bury her dead. 11.30 p.m. Crawl out in the dark, winding in and out of the ships once more en route for the beachhead.

January 31. Arrived Anzio without incident. Terrific bombardment by our guns on the beach. A foggy morning rather curtailed Jerry's activity in the air, thank goodness, and he only gave us a short air attack. We loaded 295 cases by 2 p.m. The cruiser *Spartan* lay bottom upwards by our side, having been struck by an aerial torpedo yesterday. A large Liberty ship loaded with ammunition was hit – 8 men were killed, but all the rest got off her before she blew up. She is now burning furiously.

Working in the wards all day, and been operating with Sid tonight. Passed the *Leinster* on her way up to Anzio at midnight. Lit up like a glorious gin palace – expect we look the same to her. Just made my final night round – every cot, every alleyway, the smoke room, and outside the dining room, all crowded with exhausted, shattered men – some blinded, some sleeping, some delirious, some merely restless, but no one complaining. Scots Guards, Irish Guards, County Regiments, Gunners, Americans, and German prisoners of war.

February 1. Disembarked all our patients in Naples by mid-day. Sneaked out for lunch at the Officers' Club – picked up by our boat at 4 p.m.
8.30 p.m. Sailed for Anzio once more.

February 2. Dropped anchor fairly close in to Anzio harbour. The ancient port of Nero – greeted almost at once by some heavy shells landing not far from us. All our ambulance boats gone on to the beach. Deuce of a racket going on inland, continuous, but so far has not come to much (touching wood). All loaded by 2 p.m. 291 cases, mostly Yanks. No incident, except for one dive bomber who came almost vertically down out of the sun,

and dropped his stuff unpleasantly close. Two cruisers firing just north of us, in support of land troops, are covering their action by smokescreen.
11 p.m. Signal received from H.C. *Julian* that she was in collision with another ship. Steamed up to her as she was only 4 miles ahead. No damage very much to her, so we went on.

February 3. Naples by 12.30 a.m. and disembarked in the morning. Sailed 8 p.m.

February 4.    Anzio by daybreak, embarked 221 cases – very rough and impossible to load more. One of our boats was holed hoisting, in breaking seas. Sea and wind rose, and as we were travelling westward at speed we caught the N.W. gale on the beam. Operating difficult – the chains which fixed the operating table to the floor pulled out, and the table collapsed on the floor. The anaesthetic apparatus broke loose, and the heavy cylinders were charging round, carrying everything before them. The instrument table fell on its side, and all the sterile instruments fell on the floor. In the wards all the patients were vomiting their guts out, the sloping floors made it impossible for the orderlies to reach them in time. The chest cases became cyanosed with vomiting and fright, secondary haemorrhages started. I was reduced to crawling round with a morphia syringe and doping them all into tranquillity. A temptation not to dope oneself into escape from a scene of hell let loose. Later, as we turned southward, we got the sea astern, and things were better.

February 5.   Disembarked our patients at Naples. We have had a reprieve from going to sea tonight and may get even another night of peace.

February 6-7. Ashore in Naples, and visited the Castel Elmo, where the Yanks have an A.A. station. They are still using the German and Italian AA gun which they left in position. The dungeons are full of AA shells left by them in their hurried retreat. One young platoon officer in the Loyals told me that when he was up at the Anzio beachhead he landed with the assault troops, and later was sent out on a raid to obtain prisoners. He only had about 12 men, whom he deployed in extended order. He gave the centre group old tin cans with bits of metal, and sent a man far out on the flank, each with a whistle. They advanced in the dark, shouting at the top of their voices, and beating on the cans with the metal, reducing the Jerries, who were already jumpy, to hysterics. Then the men on the flanks started blowing their whistles, and Jerry knew it was all up and that he was surrounded. They all came out with their hands up – much to their chagrin, and then it was too late, they realised that some 30-40 of them had surrendered to a mere handful of grinning British Tommies.

February 8. Dropped anchor at Anzio at 8.30 a.m. Things lively ashore, with the Jerries' long-awaited counter attack – roar of guns – crump of bursting shells and bombs, a pall of smoke lying over the country. Every now and again a shell comes screaming over us, and lands on the beach or sea. A sharp bombing attack while our boats were in harbour gave a most unpleasant time. Something, either a bomb or shell, fell into the sea about 50 yards from the ship, but luckily did not explode. The old Jerry has obviously driven our troops back and making things decidedly hot. Loaded 305 cases, and glad to leave by mid-day. Travelling down at 17 knots reached Naples before midnight. Carried a New Zealand officer who was captured in Libya two years ago, and in a prison camp near Boulogne. He escaped 2½ months ago, and has only just reached our lines. He travelled along the mountains with 4 other men. The Italians in the North are afraid to help our escaping prisoners, as the penalty is a heavy one if caught, and the reward £20 if they produce a prisoner. On their way south they ran into an Italian girl in the Secret Service, who had been collecting information for the Allies. She was also making her way southward. Our New Zealander seems to have fallen for her – with her courage and beauty she was irresistible. Hearing of our landing at Anzio they made up their minds to contact our troops. On the night of February 6 they passed through the German lines. Although fired on they were unhurt, but coming up to the American outposts they were greeted by a hail of bullets before they could make themselves known. All were hit, and the four companions killed. The beautiful Italian girl was shot through the heart. The New Zealander alone survived, with a bullet through the leg.

February 9.  Naples. Went ashore to the Opera, and heard *Madame Butterfly*.

February 10-11.  Out in the bay with cruisers, *Penelope, Dido, Mauritius, Orion* and two French destroyers. All held up by a disastrous gale.

February 12.  Sailed for Anzio at 8 p.m. Weather improved.

February 13.  Dropped anchor just outside Anzio at 8 a.m. Greeted by a fierce air attack, which nearly made me swallow my tooth water, which I was gargling. An L.C.T. brought us out some 170 cases, which we got safely on board. Meanwhile heavy German gun was shelling the beach about ½ mile away. Without any further warning the gun was switched on to the harbour entrance, where L.S.T.s, L.C.I.s and C.C.T. and amphibians were pouring forth their cargoes of troops, guns, vehicles and ammunition. The old *Dinard* was well plastered with shells. The sea was driven high into the air with vast waterspouts, bits of

H.E. shell surging and pinging in all directions, and the deafening uproar shook us all to the core. The ship was nicely bracketed with a near miss 10 yards short, and the next overshot her by 20 yards. The decks were littered with fragments, and the metalwork dented, and all covered with spray. Eventually we picked up the anchor, and moved out ¼ mile.

Arriving back in Naples we ran into another air-raid. What a day! We have many patients from Scots and Grenadier Guards, and they say our casualties are enormous – most battalions reduced to about 100 men. The C.C.S., being between an ammunition dump and A.A. battery, had another bombing last night. Casualties have been heavy in M.O.'s and Sisters and orderlies, and the scenes in the wards have been ghastly, with fellows fixed in bed in plasters, with only a bit of canvas tent round. The Germans have lost heavily, too, but our troops, supplies, ammunition and guns are all so concentrated that they can make the whole beachhead hell upon earth.

February 14. Disembarked our patients by midday. Lunched at the Club and sailed again for Anzio at 8 p.m., taking with us Major Gen. Sir E. Cowell, Brigadier Gen. Galloway and General Martin, U.S.A.

February 15. Sunny morning, very cold, and all the mountains covered with snow. A few bombs and shells did their best to disturb us, but after Sunday we are fairly hardened. The minesweepers are out sweeping a channel north of Anzio, and they were soon followed by a destroyer screen for the cruisers. The U.S. cruiser *Brooklyn* we could recognise. They darkened the air with virulent smoke before bombarding the coast. Aircraft busy, and dog fighting at about 20,000 feet was going on frequently. Embarked 207 cases by midday. The wireless says there is a lull in the fighting.

February 16. Disembarked casualties. Had a day out in Naples – lunch at Officers' Club, E.N.S.A., and tea at the Y.W.C.A.

February 17. Sailed 8 p.m. for Anzio, with American Colonel and psychologist. Mock trial in evening before Mr Justice Squires, K.C., R.A.M.C., S.P.A.M.

February 18. Arrived Anzio 7.30 a.m. and anchored outside harbour. Shell fire very heavy, into the harbour, the town, and also among the ships. The Jerries had also laid many mines in the sea overnight. A tug blew up 100 yards from us. One of our sea ambulances, returning from the harbour with the O.C. on board, went to the rescue, and brought 6 survivors to the ship, some with severe wounds. Then one of the amphibians blew up. The concussion and blast from the mines were terrific. The mines, curiously, do not explode for every ship that passes over them, but seemed to be timed for, say, the 5th ship, so that the minesweepers fail to sweep them, and every ship is lulled into a sense of false security. However we safely embarked 253 cases, and didn't we hop it! The German pressure on our troops on land is very heavy, and many of our cases have been wounded not only in action, but also in the C.C.S.s. Whatever the B.B.C. may say about the Allied line holding firm, there is no doubt that we have been pushed back closer to the sea. The beachhead is getting hotter every day, both on the land and sea, and 5th Army at Cassino is still no nearer to relieving it.

February 19. Safely berthed in Naples at 7.30 a.m. and evacuated our patients. Some letters arrived for us, some as recent as February 5, but, alas, none for me. Every officer and Sister has got from 2 to 6 letters, but poor me none. Have consoled myself with 2 kilos of oranges. The ship's company all a bit depressed by the news of the loss of the cruiser *Penelope* on her way up to

Anzio last night. It appears uncertain whether she was mined or torpedoed. She was hit in the bows, and 20 minutes later in the stern, and sank in a few minutes with heavy loss of life. We had patients from an L.S.T. that was also sunk by a mine. We have to sail again tonight, as the *Julian* appears still out of action and the *Leinster* has a cracked piston. We feel rather hardly put upon, but the casualties are many, and must be got away from these few square miles of shelled and blasted beachhead.

February 21. Held in Naples by water in the oil bunkers. Shipping losses at Anzio increasing, with the introduction of German submarines and mines. Two cruisers sunk, and two more out of action, including the cruiser *Dido*. L.S.T. torpedoed, and freight sunk. German attack held on the road from Anzio – Caroceto – Rome, 3,000 yards S. of Caroceto. A costly operation, both in men on land, and in ships, and still no end to it in sight. 56th British Division reinforced the 1st before the attack.

February 22. Sailed for Anzio at 8 p.m. on a calm night.

February 23. Arrived Anzio at 8 a.m. Wind and sea risen in the night, loading at the moment appears impossible, even the minesweepers who are trying to keep the harbour entrance clear have had to give up. All craft having a deuce of a time, with the surf beating on beach, and the seas breaking far out from the land. Ordered back to Naples.

February 24. Stayed tied up along shore in Naples all night. A great treat, as the C.O., Alec, Matron and I went to the E.N.S.A. A Quiet Weekend. Great show.

February 25. Sailed 8 p.m. for Anzio, and rolling like old boots before we have left the Bay. The wind rose to gale force, and sea got up in the night, and by 1 a.m. there was the hell of a sea battering, making further progress impossible. The old ship was standing on her beam ends and lying on her side, and there was no rest for anybody. At 2.a.m. the Captain decided to try to turn the ship.

February 26.   The first attempt failed, but the second was successful. The difficulty was that all the coast round here is hostile, and that meant a 5 hour journey before we could get shelter from the storm.

February 27.   Ordered once more to Anzio, but stopped again by the gale.

February 28.   S.E. gale still holding us up.

February 29.   Sailed for Anzio 8 p.m. Still a bit of a swell.

March 1.   Sea and wind rising in the night brought us to the beachhead with breaking waves, a howling gale, and torrential rain. Minesweepers desperately trying to keep the sea clear. A.A. ships rolling about, and destroyers almost showing their keels. Meanwhile, Jerries were plastering the sea with heavy shells. Having waited in vain for about three hours in the hope that the storm would abate and allow us to lower some boats, we were ordered to return to Naples. A filthy journey back, with a big sea striking us about abeam. For the 3rd time in my life I was sea-sick, but nobody knows!

March 2.   Pestered by enemy planes. Think they must be laying mines.

March 3.   Sailed for Anzio at 8 p.m.

March 4. After a rough night anchored in front of Anzio harbour at 8 p.m. 9.30 moved out a bit farther, shelling of shipping a bit hot, very choppy sea, but making an attempt to load if possible. We eventually loaded 136 cases. Most difficult from an L.C.T. It crashed into the side of the ship with the rending of timbers. Its guns mounted on the rear platforms kept bashing into the bottom of the boats. Then the ropes holding the L.C.T. to the ship broke, and we nearly lost some men in the sea as the two ships parted. While this struggle was going on the waves were beating over the deck of the L.C.T where all the fellows were lying on stretchers. The Jerries were plastering the sea and the ships with long range gunfire. In case we had not enough to cope with, an enemy plane came down and dropped a few bombs. Fortunately a destroyer which was standing by gave him a packet with all her guns. This kept the plane high, but not deterred – it circled for another attack. Suddenly, out of the blue, two Spitfires dropped on it like hawks on a sparrow, and we left them to it. We had our hands full. We may be holding the beachhead, but what a price and only possible by the guts of the fellows on shore holding the Jerries from breaking through right to the beach itself. This they could do in a matter of minutes if the infantry relaxed their determination. The naval craft are magnificent. The larger ships bombard the coast, the destroyers, patrol craft, and M.L. and minesweepers have to beat off the evening air attacks, protect shipping from attacks by U-boats, and keep the sea clear of mines – and at the same time bear the brunt of the enemy shell fire.

March 6. Sailed for Anzio at 8 p.m. The *Leinster* returned empty last night. The *Andrew* and *Julian* seem to have developed some engine trouble, so the old *Dinard* fills the breach once more.

March 7. A fairly calm sea at last, and we dropped anchor off Anzio about 8 a.m. Able to load with ease (from two L.C.T.s) 235 cases. Sunny day, and only a few shells disturbed us.

March 8. Berthed early in Naples. In the evening invited on board the H.M.S. *Palomares*, an A.A. cruiser which was mined at Anzio and holed in the stern. They gave us a grand party, and we arrived back at 1 a.m.

March 9. Sailing along on a bright moonlit night and in a calm sea. Radio reports the sinking of the U.S. Hospital Ship *Seminole* off Philippeville – she only left Naples the other day, and must be heavily loaded. We have been in touch with the *Seminole* many times, and she gave us a party in Gib. Everyone feeling depressed. The *Julian* has a crack in her main shaft and had left for the dry dock at Taranto. This leaves only the *Leinster, St. Andrew* and ourselves.

March 10. Anchored off Anzio at 8 a.m. on a calm morning, after a somewhat disturbed night from being involved in a submarine attack on our ships going up to Anzio – shell fire and depth charges persistent. Loaded 267 cases by 11.15 a.m. and sailed for Naples. Only a few shells and bombs fell while we were there. Arriving back in Naples for air-raid at 1.30 a.m. and another at 3.30 a.m.

March 11. Two nights running without much sleep and a hard day's work making everyone a bit tired. However, a spring-like morning, a safe return once more from Anzio. Thoughts of letters seem to have keyed up everyone's spirits to a high level. The *Seminole* has been picked up by wireless during night so we can assume that the report that she was sunk was untrue. Alas, no letters – but Alec and I went to lunch with the Captain of the A.A. cruiser *Palomares*. Very exclusive lunching in his private flat below the bridge. Went to see Rope at the garrison theatre.

March 12. Disturbed night again, with more enemy planes hovering over us dropping mines. Alongside a big American ship unloading ammunition, so we all felt very uncomfortable. Sailing postponed tonight, so perhaps we will get some sleep.

March 13. Sailed for Anzio at 8 p.m. Although calm to start with the wind rose to gale force and a heavy sea swept the ship by midnight. Uneventful passage otherwise, except for a plane which descended on us at mast-high level. Everyone's hair stood on end as we waited for a bomb, but nothing happened. The *St. Andrew*, who was coming up with us, retired in the face of the storm, but "old *Dinard* of Dunkirk and the beaches" held her course.

March 14. Dropped anchor at Anzio at 8 a.m. with a hell of a racket going on ashore. Very rough, but we managed to get 145 cases on board from an L.C.T. The latter crashed into the sides of the ship, and the prominent bows kept beating against the bottom of our boats. One of the big hawsers parted with a ping, and we parted company. Meanwhile Jerry assisted us by landing a few shells into the sea and on the beach. A fine old picnic. Now making for Naples at 18 knots. The engineer has just told me that the L.C.T. has dented in the plates into his engine room. Dropped anchor in Naples about 10 p.m.

March 15. Jennifer's birthday 10 years ago – how I wish I were home! But last night I was forcibly reminded that I was not – at 1.30 a.m. when we had been in bed only a short time, the most unholy racket started. A.A. opened up, and we thought it was only the old mine-laying Jerry coming over. We were lying out with the warships, in company with the cruisers *Orion*, *Mauritius* and "fighter *Brooklyn*" and her sister ship destroyers, hospital ships *Abba* and *St Andrew*. First the Jerries dropped flares, which lighted up every ship like daylight. The first stick of bombs fell close to our stern, one only about 20 yards away, and we felt we had been stove in. The hospital ship *Abba* had a bomb on her, killing patients, sisters, and orderlies. This was the heaviest raid on Naples for months. The little tug that generally comes to tie up in the hospital ship berths at night was hit and sunk. The G2 General Hospital was hit, and had many casualties. 100 Italian civilians were killed by one bomb. We had 8 bombs in all, very close to our ship, but apart from the concussion and rain of splinters, and A.A. and cannon shell, we escaped unharmed. We all felt rather aggrieved to return from Anzio to this!

March 16. Sailed for Anzio 8 p.m. as the *Leinster* has some supposed engine trouble, the *Andrew* some feeble reason for not going. Anzio does not seem very popular!

March 17. Anchored at Anzio at 8 a.m. after a very disturbed night. The sea route between us and the land was alive with shell fire, A.A., and flares. At 6.30 a.m. some heavy bombs were dropped close to us. Loaded 254 cases by midday from two L.C.T.s, meanwhile Jerry did his best to upset us with some long-range shell fire. Patrol craft hit and sunk during the night, and a L.S.T. yesterday. We don't like Anzio!

March 18. Berthed in Naples at 7.30 a.m., and disembarked our patients. Everyone a bit depressed, repairs have at last been granted, and we are to lie up in Naples. The officers can take a night or two off if they can get away. Next, a mail has arrived, with 4 letters from O. – one has taken only 7 days. Next – a letter from War Office classifying me as a Graded Surgeon from 17 December 1943. Next – we are to be given the 1939-43 Star, for six months operations in dangerous waters. Everyone on the top of the world.

March 20. To the 1st New Zealand C.C.S. with the B.T.U. lorry with Sid. Interesting drive through Aversa, crossing the Volturno at Capua, very dusty, and roads crowded with lorries, guns, Bren gun carriers, and armoured cars and tanks. Nothing much doing at the F.S.U. as they cannot get the casualties out of Cassino in daylight, went on by various lifts in ammunition truck and wireless van to the M.D.S. Nothing much doing there also, so went on a few more miles to get a view of the pass of Cassino dominated by the Monastery Hill. The New Zealanders have captured all but the S.W. corner of the town, Jerries being reinforced in the town and thought to be coming up through the deep sewers. The Indians are having a tough time on the slopes of Monastery Hill, sometimes having to be supplied with food and ammo by parachute. The whole of Cassino covered in smoke pall. Incessant bombardment by our guns and Germans in a pretty hot spot. Back to Naples, to find Vesuvius in violent eruption, lava showing as red molten streams coming down the mountain, villages evacuated and overwhelmed. Flames and molten lava belching forth from the crater, and the whole sky appears on fire.

March 22. To Cercola with Dickie Rees, to see the molten streams of lava pouring down Vesuvius. The top of the church of S. Sebastiano and some of the tall buildings still show above the lava, but the rest of the village of 5,000 people is buried deep in the lava. The larval stream, about 20 feet high, advancing at a rate of 4 metres a minute.

March 23. The famous cruiser *Ajax* at anchor near us.

March 24. Hitch-hiked to Sorrento for 2 nights at the Red Cross convalescent home. The whole of the peninsula enveloped in clouds of lava dust, blotting out the sun, and making everything look dark and depressing. Saw Bobbles Herschell and took him to tea at the Y.M.C.A. at Sorrento.

March 26. Returned to ship.

March 27-30. Repairs still going on.

March 30. Lighter in collision with our bows about 9 a.m. Stove in the plates on starboard side. Great news from Ministry of War Transport that we and the *Julian* are to proceed to United Kingdom in the "immediate future". All had a tot of Chartreuse on the strength of it. Now we are all praying that we shall not get caught in air-raid in the harbour, which threatens us every night in our very exposed position.

April 2. Sailed for Anzio at 8 p.m. Calm night, and all quiet.

April 3. Anchored off the entrance to Anzio at 8 a.m. Heavy bombardment on land, and some shells on the beach. Mine blew up quite close to the ship, otherwise things fairly quiet. Embarked 252 patients by 1 a.m. and sailed for Naples at 15 knots.

April 4. Disembarked our patients and moved out to anchor in the Bay of Pozzuoli on a lovely evening, with a Turner sunset over Bacoli.

April 5. Ordered back to Naples at 12.30 midday. Rumours that we are to proceed to Algiers on 7th or 8th en route for home, but we dare not think about it, particularly as we are back in the most vulnerable place for air attack.

April 6. Orders received to sail at 9 a.m. tomorrow for Algiers – excitement intense.

April 7. Marvellous sunny morning, calm blue sea, and we have now left Naples 100 miles behind us. Just swerved in time to miss a mine an hour ago. Three swallows accompanying us and having a rest. We are trying to feed them, but they are too scared to eat.

April 9. Berthed Algiers.

April 11. Inspection by Maj. General Hartgill D.M.S. B.N.A.C., who thanked us for the magnificent work which we and all the hospital carriers had done. We could hold our heads very high when we returned to England with the thought of the vital link which we had supplied in combined operations, in landings on enemy territory, etc. Our heads and chests swelled visibly. As the General was going one of his buttons flew off and he had to get one of the sisters to sew it on. To dinner in the evening with the *Empire Clyde*. Heavy air attack on a convoy just outside the harbour shook us all to the core at this vital stage of our journey. Yankee destroyer hit amidships by an aerial torpedo, but two tugs, one an ocean-going naval tug, gallantly went out and brought her in (somewhat mangled) to the berth next to us, with 20 dead on board.

April 13. Ashore in the morning to buy a few more presents. 7 p.m. left Algiers, westward bound for Gib.

April 15. Anchored in Gib. at 8.30 a.m. No shore leave, as smallpox is rampant. Filled with oil and water, the new bunker under G. ward filled with 90 tons of oil, bringing the old ship's nose down a bit, but it gives us 3 days extra at 12 knots. Sailed at 3 p.m. on last lap with our fingers crossed for England.

April 16. Cape St Vincent abeam at 1 p.m., and a roughish N. Westerly sea.

April 18. A calm day. At midday wireless message to proceed to Falmouth, and there to be routed for Southampton. Excitement intense, and speed increased to 17 knots. Party in the Sergeants' Mess pretty lively, ending up by some funny people hosing my bed through the porthole at 3 a.m., and then smashing the crash panel in my door.

April 19. 10 miles S of the Bishop Rock at 9 a.m. Falmouth by 2 p.m. – on a pouring wet day, and a cold wind.

April 20. Sailed for Southampton at 7 a.m. Travelling all out.

# Chapter 13

# Home Again

As soon as I got ashore at Southampton I took a train to London, went across to Paddington and got a train to Didcot where Maud and Jack Reeves, who lived at the surgery in Church Street, came to meet me. How exciting it was to see friendly Wantage faces again – and how remote it seemed from the beaches at Anzio.

O. and the children, all rather out of action from a wretched attack of chickenpox, had hung big Union Jacks out of the windows to greet my return. The only physical taste of war that Wantage had felt was a bomb dropped on a field near the gasworks – it was assumed to have been a stray bomb meant for the airfield at Abingdon. Nanny had been taking the children for a walk along the Denchworth Road when there was a loud bang, and sound of an aeroplane overhead. Jennifer, who had been pushing the pram with Dick in it, made an instant decision on the best course of action – she turned round and started running for home, still pushing the pram. Nanny was left with no choice but to run after them. Asked when she got home what she had felt about the bomb she said calmly, "Well, my first thought was to put up the hood of the pram."

Poor Nanny – that was the second shock the war had brought her. We had a number of Americans stationed in Wantage during the war, and they built an airfield nearby to be used for the eventual airborne invasion of France. They used to use the footpath alongside our house as a short cut to the Nissen huts where they were billeted, and were sometimes quite rowdy on their way back to camp after the pubs had closed. One night, when it was nearly midnight and Nanny was sleeping in the front bedroom with Dick in the other bed, she was woken by the door opening. The light was switched on, and there was a large American standing, swaying slightly, in the doorway. "Hello babe" he said. Nanny sat up in bed and tried to say something but she was so frightened that she just opened her mouth and nothing came. Eventually she managed to gasp "You can't come in here, you might wake up the child."

I think the sight of Nanny sitting up in bed with her night cap and ginger wig made the American realise, even in his drunken state, that she was not the tender young chick he was looking for. Nanny's honour was saved by the evacuee, Aubrey, who took the man firmly by the arm, led him on to the footpath, and set him in the right direction for his camp as he swayed off into the night.

It was wonderful to see the children again, and it seemed hard to realise that they were the same children I had left a year ago – they were so much bigger than the pictures I had of them in my memory. There were still a few bottles of claret in the cellar, so I opened one of them, and stayed up with O. getting and giving news until the early hours of next morning. There was so much to say that neither of us knew where to begin or end.

We had been told on the way home that the *Dinard* was going back to the Channel, to be used for ferrying casualties when the Second Front that everybody was now waiting for was opened. We all knew that an assault on the German-held coast of Western Europe must come, but, of course, nobody – outside the Chiefs of Staff – knew where or when. D-Day was, in fact, still some months away, and anyway, I had two weeks' leave to enjoy.

But I did a good deal of thinking on my leave, and decided that since I was chiefly interested in surgery, my skills would be better employed at a proper hospital rather than in the first-aid work of a hospital ferry. The late Sir Ralph Glyn, who was then M.P. for our Division, lived nearby, and was a friend of mine. So I went to see him with my problem. He got in touch with the War Office, and was able to get me transferred to the 4th Field Hospital at Hambledon, near Southampton.

The 4th Field Hospital was in buildings that had been formerly a home for sub-normal girls run by a convent. The place, known as Coldeast Hospital, had been taken over by the army and re-equipped in readiness for the invasion. To start with, there was not much for me to do, and I had a fairly quiet time, concerned with routine day-to-day surgery, mostly hernias and appendicitis. It was obvious, however, that this was merely a lull in the war. There was constant activity in the Solent, and we could see huge mysterious rafts of concrete being towed about the place – we learned later that these were pieces of the famous Mulberry Harbour, designed to form an artificial port for the landings on the Normandy beaches. Troops were constantly assembling near Southampton, but they were not allowed to mix with people in the town.

O. was able to come down, sometimes for weekends. The hospital was extremely short of living space, and we used to sit lingering over dinner in the Officers' Mess – the bar was so cramped that there was nowhere else to sit. We used to sit so long over dinner that sometimes the orderlies turned out the lights to get rid of us.

One sad night a flying bomb landed almost directly on the Wrens' quarters near the hospital, where they were having a dance. The blast of the explosion shook our buildings, and we rushed out to an appalling sight – bodies and bits of bodies of girls wearing dance frocks. It seemed so much worse for being out of context – this was not a battlefront, but a place where girls were dancing.

By the middle of June 1944 we began to get really busy. Our hospital was not due to receive the first waves of casualties, and our first load of severe cases came to us by accident – an ambulance launch bringing about 100 men ashore ran aground almost in front of the hospital. It was like the old days on the *Dinard* with the same dreadful decisions to make – whether to deal first with a man groaning with pain from shrapnel sticking out of his thigh, or to try to treat a man with a bullet wound in the abdomen, which you knew must have penetrated the bowel to cause peritonitis. Oddly, one of my very first cases was not due to wounds at all, but an acute appendicitis. A young soldier had gone over in a landing craft that morning with a slight tummy pain, but he had not thought much of it, and did not want to leave his mates. He was a bit sick on the way over, but again he hadn't thought much of it – a lot of men were seasick. He landed and tried to go forward from the beach, but his pain became acute, and he collapsed. By the time he got to me the appendix was gangrenous, and he was in desperate need of surgery, which, mercifully, was able to save his life.

Once we started to get busy, we worked all round the clock. I recall starting to operate on Wednesday evening, and carrying on with scarcely a break until I collapsed into bed on Saturday morning. In typical army fashion, that was the morning when some top brass decided to inspect the hospital. So I had to get up and go round with them – and kept nodding off to sleep when they asked me questions about the patients.

A sad casualty of the Normandy beaches was the gallant old *Dinard* She was back at her old job, moving in to collect the wounded, when she struck a mine. She did not sink, but was severely damaged, and had to be towed backwards across the Channel – a gaping hole in her bows made it impossible for her to go ahead. I saw her being brought into the Solent, and felt that she had really served humanity well.

As the war moved on from the Normandy beaches our work fell off. Hospitals were established in France, and it was decided that Coldeast Hospital had done its job. So it was handed back to the convent, and I was posted again to the Cambridge Hospital at Aldershot. There my job was to deal with the day to day surgery of the less acute cases. I learned a lot about hernias, doing about twelve a week.

One evening a casualty came in, a chap who had been larking about in a bar and had suffered a Colles fracture of his wrist. I wanted to set it, so I went to the Mess, and asked if anyone there would help me by giving a quick anaesthetic. A man named Charles Seward immediately volunteered, and when we had finished setting the fracture we retired to the bar for a chat. There I discovered that Charles had a brother, Edgar, also a doctor, who had done a locum in the practice at Wantage. That meeting was the beginning of a lifelong friendship. I found Charles very good company, always ready to help with anything, and with a grand sense of humour.

Towards the end of 1944 it began to look as if the war with Germany would soon be over. My sense of heartfelt thankfulness, however, was rapidly succeeded by a sense of gloom with the news that I was about to be posted to Burma. I felt that I had done my bit in two wars, and I just didn't want to go to Burma. I had to undergo a medical examination for Far East service – and the doctor who examined me was Charles Seward. Perhaps we were a bit naughty, but Charles did find a bit of shrapnel still in my thigh from the First World War, and a damaged lumbar vertebra from a hunting accident. I was also able to say truthfully that I suffered from chronic sinusitis. Anyway, Charles's report was that I was unfit for Far East service. This had to go before the Colonel, and I asked him what he thought. He replied, "Frankly, it stinks, but we'll see what we can do for you." The upshot was that instead of going to Burma I was posted to a hospital in Brussels.

I had a week's embarkation leave before going over the Channel again to Ostend, where there was a transit camp and train loads of troops bound for the front. We stayed three nights at Bruges, sleeping on a factory floor with one blanket. It certainly was cold even with all one's clothes on, or maybe the old campaigner was getting soft. Anyway, wandering round the town and visiting the Cathedral made up for the discomforts of the night.

I don't know why, but I did not like the atmosphere in that hospital in Brussels. It had a curious arrangement of stairs. All around the building there was an inclined plane, so that if one wanted to go into the ward above one had to go outside, up the ramp, and then inside again.

The base hospital was about 10 miles outside Brussels, and we spent many happy evenings at the Officers' Mess in the centre of Brussels. This was a palatial house with magnificent rooms and chandeliers, where the Duchess of Richmond had the Officers Ball on the night before the Battle of Waterloo. One night when I got back to the hospital after a trip to the Officers' Mess, I was told that there was a young lad who needed treatment in the casualty department. I went down and saw a man of about 25 in a very shocked condition. He had tried to get on to a crowded train, had jumped at the tail board, but had been unable to scramble on. A train in the opposite direction came by and hit him. He had a fractured pelvis, with masses of bleeding in the large muscles. His was one of the most serious cases we received, and it took some time before his condition improved.

After a few weeks I was posted from Brussels to Duffel hospital, nearer the front. This had been an old workhouse, run by nuns. The pace was hotter here, and we received many casuaties, not only from the front line, but also civilians. We had one girl of 12 years old, with severe burns, whose dressings I had to change every fifth day. She was a sweet uncomplaining child, and I used to give her 1/6th gr. morphia before I changed them. In spite of all we could do, however, she died. Her death upset me greatly – how cruel war is when an innocent child of twelve dies because politicians argue.

We had a lucky escape one night when a V2 rocket came over and landed right in the middle of the grounds between two buildings. But the ground was soft, and the rocket-head sank in without exploding. There would have been little left of the hospital if it had gone off.

I enjoyed my time at Duffel, particularly because Colonel Muir, whom I had met at Aldershot, was working there. I respected his surgical skills, and I learnt an enormous lot from him. I recognised that I could never have the finesse of the great surgeons, but, with my varied experience, I did know my exact limitations, and I would never take on more than I was capable of coping with efficiently. Colonel Muir appreciated this, and gave me great encouragement.

Another of my friends from the Cambridge Hospital came out to Duffel, John Evans, the E.N.T. specialist. He was feeling frustrated because his instruments had been posted to a hospital farther down the line. We had just had a slight reprimand from the C.O. of the camp that our discipline was falling below army standards, and we were told that we were expected to salute fellow officers. Soon afterwards, I was walking to the main block when John Evans came across the courtyard, followed by the CO. My hand snapped up into a salute. John Evans did not realise that the C.O. was behind him, and replied with a very rude two fingers sign to show what he thought of pompous army discipline. That caused some trouble, and we were sent off like naughty school children for a good dressing down.

But the end of the war was getting close and we veterans – I was fifty by now – were sent back to Normandy, to a place called Tomnai. Things were more relaxed here, and I was put in charge of the Officers Mess. We were expecting what was left of the

German High Command to surrender any day, and I wanted to get in sufficient drink for a decent celebration. I contacted the Town Mayor, who had the job of looking after the smooth running of the town. He was a pompous little chap, with a very large stomach, and he said that he would come with me in an open staff car to collect some drink. It was while we were loading this into the car that news of the German surrender came through. The whole town went wild and rushed into the streets. The little Mayor responded with great excitement, ordering his driver to go slowly while he stood up in the back of the car waving to the crowd as they threw bouquets at us. At the precise moment that someone threw a huge bunch of peonies the car jerked forward. The peonies hit the Mayor in the chest and I can see him now, disappearing backwards into the bottom of the car, shouting "Take over, Squires".

We had a riotous party that evening, with everyone wondering how soon they could get home. While awaiting my discharge I stayed at a convent in Bayeux, which had been converted into a hospital. We were looked after very well by the nuns, who cooked us magnificent meals. There was one nun who had spent her childhood in Ireland, growing up with horses, and she loved to talk into the early hours of the morning about her experiences.

At last I was told to report to Antwerp for my embarkation papers. I was lucky in getting a lift in a jeep with all my kit. The night before I crossed the Channel we were sent a batman to help us with our packing. I wanted to do my own pack but when I got to my room I found that it had already been done: it was not until I arrived at Folkestone the next day that I found that half my things had been stolen. I was ashamed of myself – old campaigner caught out on his very last day of military services.

The army gave us a grand farewell feast in the transit camp at Folkestone before sending us on by train to Guildford for official demobilisation. There were vast queues of soldiers waiting to go through the checkpoints, and everyone was given a farewell present of civilian clothes – pants, vest, shirt, socks, shoes and a blue serge suit. As we walked away we were besieged by spivs, offering us £10 a parcel, which they would resell on the black market.

And so I went back to Didcot, where I was met by O. who was expecting her third baby in a week's time and could only just fit her large tummy under the steering wheel. The children had again decorated the front windows of the house with the old Union Jacks, and the hall with streamers saying "Welcome Home".

## Chapter 14

# After the War and the National Health Service

How strange it seemed to be back in Wantage after having been away for so long! Wantage (save for the one bomb which had dropped near the gasworks and frightened our Nanny) had been spared most of the physical horrors of war. But the blackout, ration books, shortages of everything, all the dreariness of wartime existence had, of course, afflicted Wantage as much as anywhere else. People were very, very tired. There were some physical changes in the town – the iron railings that had stood around the churchyard, and in front of my house, all the time I had known the place were gone: they had been taken away to be melted down and turned into armaments. Painting and decorating had been all but impossible for six years, and the town was looking sadly shabby.

But the war was over, and that huge relief made up for everything else. In some ways, too, the demands of war had actually made life better for people. There had been completely full employment, with work for women as well as men, for half a decade. And food rationing had not only worked brilliantly, but had ensured a fairer distribution of essential foods than had ever been achieved in Britain before. Dull as it may have been, I am sure that the basic food that people ate during the war was more nutritious than much of the stuff that housewives are seduced into buying nowadays by television advertisements.

It had been a hard war for women in O.'s position. She had had to cope with our own two young children as well as two evacuees in a large house, with very little help. Before the war we had employed a cook, a parlourmaid, two gardeners, and a groom. As the war went on, O. had nobody. True to form, she managed wonderfully well. And she discovered that there are even some advantages in having to do everything on one's own. If she just didn't feel like eating in the evening, or wanted only a snack, she could do whatever she liked without having to worry about hurting the cook's feelings.

Our third child, another daughter, was born that year. O. went into the Acland nursing home at Oxford for her confinement, and after the anxiety of her two previous confinements it was an immense relief to feel that the antibiotics developed during the war were available against infection. I called our daughter Judy after my favourite Alsatian, who had died just before the war.

It was reassuring to discover how pleased my patients were to see me again, and after I had been back at work for a few weeks I felt that I had been hardly away at all. I had had the same feeling on coming back from France in the First World War, and again on my return from Australia. One would meet the same man in the same grocer's shop, see the same man in the same garage, and think "How boring for the poor chap – he is in exactly the same place as when I left him." But suppose a traveller passing through Wantage in 1924 had had a sudden stomach pain – he would have seen Dr Squires at his Church Street surgery. And suppose the same man had again been taken ill in Wantage in 1966 – he would have seen the same Dr Squires in the same surgery. And he might think, "Poor man – he has been sitting in exactly the same place for over 40 years." How little we know of other people's lives.

I had not been back at work long before I realised that I

needed to make some changes in myself. When my first maternity patients came along after the war I felt that two years of dealing with shrapnel and gunshot wounds had left me distinctly rusty on the gynaecological side of medicine. So I determined to work for the diploma of the Royal College of Gynaecologists. I studied hard, and then went up to London to take the exam. I was at least twice the age of the other candidates, and when I got to the examination hall I was taken for one of the invigilators, and shown into their sitting room.

This was sorted out, and I coped with the written papers. Then came the viva voce part of the exam, in which we had to examine a patient, and answer questions put to us by the examiners. One of the examiners was an old friend of mine from Oxford. His colleague, who had been questioning me, turned to him and said, "Do you wish to ask Dr Squires any questions about this patient?" "Good heavens, no," said my friend. "Dr Squires has delivered far more babies than I have!"

So I got my diploma, and felt that at least as far as maternity cases were concerned I was reasonably up to date.

Those first years after the war were dominated by the coming into being of the National Health Service. Whatever good the NHS may have done – and it has certainly done much – it was introduced in a morass of political bitterness. I attended many meetings of the British Medical Association at which the negotiations were discussed, and it became more and more apparent that General Practitioners were getting a rough deal. Mr Aneurin Bevan (then Minister of Health, and pilot of the NHS Bill through Parliament) may have considered it politically astute to divide the profession by making huge concessions to the hospital consultants, but he distorted the practice of medicine in Britain. The Labour Government's strategy was to win over the consultants, and to ignore as far as possible the G.P.s – the final terms were settled without the consent of the G.P.s. Financially, we came out of the negotiations extremely badly. We had all had to buy our practices – or shares in them – and the normal rate was two years' purchase; that is, if a practice was earning £3,000 a year, you paid £6,000 for it. The Government refused to give us more than 1½ years' purchase; moreover, they valued practices as they were just after the war, when most of them were run down. Harsher still, the Government insisted that no money could actually be paid to a G.P. until he retired – which, in my case, was 20 years ahead. So not only were we robbed at a stroke of 25% of our savings which had gone into buying practices, but the money, when it was paid, was worth very much less than when it was taken from us. The interest of 1% which was allowed on unpaid money for our practices was little more than an insult.

To rub salt into our wounds, we began getting letters from insurance companies offering to buy our entitlement to our money for cash at an enormous discount (the insurance company, of course, gambling on how long it would have to wait). In my case I was offered cash at the rate of £2,500 for £4,000.

It was sad that legislation which was so unsordid in its ideals should have led to so much sordid swindling of the doctors who had to make it work.

The downgrading of the G.P. in the NHS affected the attitude of young doctors as they qualified. Instead of regarding General Practice as a good career to enter, they began to think of it only as something to fall back upon if they could not make the grade in hospital medicine. A G.P. who needed a partner in the early days of the NHS often had great difficulty in finding anyone who was any good.

The tradition of General Practice had always been that a doctor took full responsibility for his patient, calling in a specialist, or inviting a second opinion, as he deemed necessary in the interests of his patient. Now, we were reduced to the job of merely sorting out patients for the hospital specialists – who might often be far less experienced than the G.P. There were strict limits to the requests that we ourselves might make to hospitals. We were allowed to ask for "simple investigations", such as blood counts, but if we felt that a patient needed, say, an X-ray after a barium meal to investigate an abdominal complaint, the request had to be sanctioned by a "specialist". This was such a time-wasting process for the patient, requiring endless hanging about at the hospital to which he presented our letter that patients sometimes decided to do without investigations that they ought to have had. Things are better now. We can request X-rays ourselves and present the patient to the specialist with an X-ray accompanying our diagnosis, so that the specialist does not have to waste either his own time or the patient's, but can use his skill to determine what form of treatment, medical or surgical, he considers best.

Another trouble of those early days of the NHS was the flood of patients who came to us with trivialities merely to get their "free" medicine. Memory may be a little deceitful here. If you have seen, perhaps, sixty patients in a day, and one was unpleasant and abused your service, it is that one whom you remember. There may have been less real abuse of the NHS than the impression that remains; nevertheless, there was certainly a good deal of abuse. My partner had to visit one patient – an elderly woman – at her home. He examined her, prescribed, and left the house. As he was shutting the gate, the woman's daughter ran up to him: could she have a prescription for a new pair of elastic stockings for her mother?

It was a cold morning, my partner had many other patients to visit, and he was a little cross at having to undo his bag, get out his prescription-pad, and write a prescription at the garden gate. "Why," he said, "didn't you ask for this when I was in the house? It would have been so much easier." "Oh, but I couldn't," she replied. "You see, I want those stockings for my mother as a Christmas present, and I don't want her to know about them."

*Charlie Seward and self enjoying a drink*

Abuse? To a busy doctor, yes, but one must be fair. From the woman's point of view it was, I suppose, a reasonable enough request. It did not occur to her how tiresome it is to write prescriptions out-of-doors, nor did she consider three or four minutes of a doctor's time as having any particular value. She could, indeed, have gone to the surgery – but why bother when the doctor had come to her house? One must regard this sort of thing as thoughtlessness rather than deliberate abuse. Unhappily, people are often thoughtless.

The year after my return from the war we decided to spend a fortnight abroad, and made first for a village on Lake Maggiore for our holiday. It was an odd feeling to go to the Continent in peace after all the destruction and restrictions I had known. Switzerland seemed blissfully peaceful, and from the balcony of our pension we could watch the steamer making its way across the lake, leaving a magnificent plume of white wake centred in a

*Glum at the Masonic Ball*

*An Hon. Surgeon to the Hunt, Dr. F. V Squires, was dancing a slow fox-trot with Miss Marjorie Pearce*

*Smart living*

picture of high mountains.

After a few days on Lake Maggiore we crossed the Alps and went to Venice. Everything there lived up to our expectations. As we entered St Mark's Square on our first night there was an orchestra playing on a gondola and the music floated over the canal, with myriad lights reflected in the water. The exchange was very much in our favour, and we managed to change all our money at about double the official

202

*Seagull*

rate. It was a lovely holiday.

O.'s father had died before the war, and we took over the house at Carbis Bay. We spent many summer holidays there, packing the house with huge parties. My dark green Wolseley 14 had survived the war sitting on wooden blocks and sometimes we would set off for expeditions with eight people in the car and four more sitting on cushions in a trailer. A particular luxury on holidays was to be able to stop at a pub for a pint of beer.

It is difficult for a doctor to visit a pub in his home town: either he will be embarrassed by feeling that his patients are hoping he will not be having a second pint before going to the

*Holding my horse by the head collar*

surgery, or he will embarrass the patients among his fellow drinkers because he knows too many intimate details of their lives.

*Harry Carvey with my horse*

I loved our Cornish holidays, and long, splendid walks on the windswept moors. The sparse trees look as though they have been trimmed with a pair of clippers, whereas in fact they have been trimmed by the savage south westerly gales. You can see the effect of gales on the roofs of farm buildings, where liquid cement has been brushed over the slates to stop the wind from tearing them away.

When the practice at Wantage had got going again I got in touch with Charles Seward, whose company I had enjoyed so much when we were both serving at the Cambridge Hospital in Aldershot. He was then working in a practice at Winchester, but he was able to leave to join us at Wantage. Our partnership was a great success, and we have remained lifelong friends. Charles is a man of fine clinical judgement, with a nice sense of humour. Nothing was ever too much trouble for him, and the patients quickly grew to like him as much as I did.

With the desperate shortages of almost everything after the war it was next to impossible to keep a horse, so I did not have one. But I missed riding very much, particularly as it would have taken my mind off some of the frustrations of the early days of the NHS. We general practitioners were not encouraged to keep up an interest in surgery, and it was difficult for us to operate as we had been accustomed to in the local hospital. If one did carry out an operation one had much to lose and very little to gain – except the personal satisfaction of being able to help a patient. Since I could hardly ever operate, and had no horse to ride, I kept my hands occupied by making model boats.

But I wanted more and more to have a horse again, and one evening, at a party at Lockinge, Mrs. Berkeley, a well-known figure in the hunting field, came over to me and said, "We haven't seen you out much lately, Dr Squires. We miss you leading the field. I have a chestnut cob you might be interested in." I couldn't resist this, so I bought Ginger from her. He was a pig of a horse, with an infuriating habit of turning round arid starting to go home as soon as one had set out on a ride.

I offered the children a prize of ten shillings for the first to ride Ginger to the Ridgeway and back. Next morning Dick got up at six o'clock, saddled Ginger and set off to win the prize. All went well for about half a mile, but just past the cemetery on the way to the Downs Ginger started turning round. The only thing Dick could do to keep him facing in the right direction was to dismount, take his head collar, and lead him. But Ginger was at his most stubborn that morning. If he couldn't return to his stable by walking forward, he would walk backwards. Dick never got him got him beyond the cemetery. By 07.00 Ginger was walking backwards down Ormond Road. By 08.00 he was walking backwards along Grove Street into the Market Square. By 08.30 he had taken the exit from the square towards the church and home. The children going to the Church of England school had a fascinating spectacle of a horse going backwards with a furious boy who could do nothing to control him. Dick, incensed by the children laughing at him, gave Ginger a whack with his riding crop, whereupon he jumped the churchyard wall and began going backwards round the gravestones. At that point Dick accepted that Ginger had won yet another round, and led him the twenty yards or so back to his stable.

Apart from this maddening habit, though, I had a lot of fun on Ginger, though he was rather like a sack of potatoes to ride. Things got a bit easier and post-war shortages were remedied, and over the years I was able to acquire two horses which I grew to love greatly, Heron and Seagull. Heron was a wonderfully steady and reliable horse. I hunted him for seven years, and he never fell with me. I used to go for an occasional day's hunting with the Heythrop in the Cotswolds, and I often went with Jan Morphew, a friend who lived at East Hendred. On one occasion I lent Heron to Jan for the day, and said that I would give him a fiver if Heron came down with him. At the end of the day we were just beyond Burford, where the hill winds up the far side of the town towards Stow-on-the-Wold. Jan said that he would have one more spin over a stone wall, but as he put Heron at the wall another horse rode in front of him. Heron refused and Jan fell off, but Heron stayed upright, so I kept my fiver.

Seagull was a huge dappled grey which I bought from a farmer in Cornwall, near Penzance – I called him Seagull to remind me of Cornwall. We had been to the Penzance Agricultural Show – on a day that was the English August at its worst. As the show jumping went on, so the wind and rain increased. The huge dappled grey was quite undaunted by the weather, and went round the ring with the calm of those old broad-backed circus horses which would plod on steadily while acrobats jumped on their backs and clowns threw pails of water over them. As this Penzance grey approached the highest fence the wind blew some hurdles in his path. Quite untroubled, he took off early and cleared the hurdles as well as the fence. I tracked him down after the show and bought him from the farmer who owned him.

    I had some wonderful days hunting and riding over the Downs on Seagull. He could jump almost anything, and never let me down. He was a wonderfully good-natured horse, as well. Every night before I went to bed I would cut a slice of bread for him and take it to him in the stable. When I gave it to him I would put my arms round his heck and he would rest his head on my shoulder, rub his muzzle on my back, and make contented noises.

One Friday night when I took his bread to him, looking forward to a good ride on Saturday, I found him breathing rapidly and shivering. I feared he had pneumonia, and praying that it was a bacterial pneumonia that would respond to an antibiotic, I gave him an injection of penicillin. I slept uneasily, and early in the morning went out to see how he was. His huge form was stretched out in the loose box, dead.

    Well, I had to send for the knacker's van to take him away but when the van came I could not bear to see him go, so I went out. My groom, tough old Harry Carvey, broke down – it was the only time I ever saw him cry. He sat in the kitchen, wearing his peaked cap, and wept unashamedly into a big spotted handkerchief.

    Harry Carvey had been groom to George Witherby, and I had known him since 1923, when he had met us with our horses in the cobbled yard of the Bear Hotel on my first visit to Wantage. He had worked at the Didcot Ordnance Depot during the war, and after the war had retired to live in Wantage, in a cottage at the end of Priory Road which he shared with his mother, a dog called Rabbit and a friend whom he had met in a pub and whom we knew only as Slippy. When I was able to have some horses again it was natural that Harry Carvey should take on the job of grooming them.

    He was a great character, and a really splendid human being.

Tremendously independent, at the age of 70 he did all his own cooking as well as looking after his mother, who was over 90, bedridden and incontinent. I never heard him moan or complain – he just got on with the job of washing out the sheets each morning.

Harry's whole life had been with horses. I had only to say that I wanted to go riding at a particular time, and he would have a horse immaculately turned out and waiting for me. He knew every copse and wood in the neighbourhood, and when the hounds drew a particular copse he knew just which way the fox would run. He had the habit that many grooms seem to have, of breathing through his teeth. I put this down to the dust particles that fly up when grooming a horse – by breathing through their teeth they trap the particles, and so are able to spit them out. He had a rich store of language, which he would use on a horse, or anyone in sight. Once I asked a neighbour's child if she liked Mr. Carvey, and she said, "I like him when he swears."

In the last years after his mother had died, Harry's only entertainment was a game of cribbage in the Woolpack Inn in Church Street; with his bandy legs and arthritic gait he would stagger there every night. One night he just did not come home. He left the Woolpack after his game of cribbage, and died of a heart attack on the way home to his cottage. There can be few who have led such useful, selfless lives.

Jan Morphew of East Hendred and I hunted together so regularly that we used to be known as The Doctor and The Doctor's Disciple! I have written already of one of our rides in Cotswolds country – we used to try to get a couple of days in the Cotswolds every season. Jan would come round for my horse early in the morning with a ramshackle old horse box that he had, and I would either travel with him and the horses in the van or, if I had some patients to see first, set off after him in the car. That van was always breaking down, and I can see old Jan now, cursing and spitting petrol as he tried to get the fuel pipe unblocked by sucking through it. One day he gave up, and took the van to a garage, where the cause of all the trouble was discovered. At some stage in the van's past the fuel cap had been lost, and had been temporarily replaced by a rolled up copy of the Daily Mail. This had slipped into the tank, and slowly disintegrated, blocking the fuel system with shreds of paper. This came to light only when the garage mechanic took off the tank to clean it.

The Cotswolds are magnificent country from a horseman's point of view. It is one of our odd national traditions that only when hunting is a private individual allowed to ride over other people's farmland and see the countryside at its closest – this is the greatest privilege and the greatest charm of hunting. You not only see, you feel part of the countryside itself; you both see and feel exactly how each field has been ploughed, you experience the rabbit warrens, you are intimately concerned with the hawthorns in the hedgerows. It is the quality of the jumps that makes a day in the Cotswolds so exciting. In the Old Berks country around Wantage many fields are hemmed in by barbed wire, and often the hawthorn hedges will have a strand of wire in them. In the Cotswolds one may have a series of perhaps twenty stone walls to fly over, each a clean and exhilarating jump. And at the end of the run the fox nearly always gets away – which always pleases me.

The Master of the Heythrop then was Ronnie Wallace, who was always very kind to me. He did not charge me a cap fee. On a gentleman's agreement I would act as medical officer and pick up any riders who might fall off.

One Saturday morning when Jan and I had arranged to go to the Cotswolds I had a call to see Lord Burghley's daughter, Victoria. Lord Burghley was then Master of the Old Berks. As usual when I was going hunting, I put on a pair of grey flannel trousers over my breeches, a sports jacket over my hunting waistcoat, and wore a shirt with a stock. Lord Burghley recognised my hunting kit under my civilian disguise, and said "See you at the meet, Squires, in about an hour's time." "Er – yes," I said, knowing that at that very moment Jan was loading Seagull into the horsebox and that we were all set for a good run into the Cotswolds.

Things turned out differently. When we got to the Cotswolds we found thick mist everywhere, and the meet was postponed in the hope of a change of weather. But the fog thickened, and after waiting for about an hour the meet was abandoned. We went back to Faringdon with our tails between our legs to join up with the Old Berks. I can feel the embarrassment now as Jan and I cantered across a field towards a copse near Baulking that was being drawn – and there were not a few remarks about the difficulties some people seem to find in tearing themselves away from pubs.

Henry was another Cornish horse. He was a chestnut gelding, which I bought from Henry Sandow, who farmed near Zennor, and I called him Henry after his former owner. The Sandow brothers, Henry and Edwin, were both farmers, with farms about three miles apart, and they were particularly kind to us on our Cornish holidays. I met them first through my son, Dick, who, as he got older, used to look for summer jobs on farms. One day Dick was helping Edwin Sandow with the harvest, pitching sheaves into a waggon, when he hurt his hand on a particularly fierce thistle. Edwin picked up another thistle and crushed it in his hand like a piece of paper, remarking "You Cockneys would have tougher hands if you worked harder with them" – everyone who came from beyond Exeter was a Cockney. Henry and Edwin used to take me riding over the Cornish moors, difficult country, strewn with granite boulders, but lovely, wild and remote. The Cornish stone fences are very different from the Cotswold walls. As in the Cotswolds the stones come from the ground when it is broken for making into fields, but the Cotswold stones tend to be flat and laminated, easy for building into dry stone walls, whereas the Cornish stones are mostly large granite boulders. These are packed into walls with earth to hold them together, and in time the earth is seeded with grass and wild plants, which help to bind the wall into a solid mass. Often these walls have a broad flat grass-covered top, and a horse jumping such a wall will tend to land on top, strike with his hind feet and then leap clear.

The Sandow brothers had some fine horses which they let me ride on the moors, and I so much liked one that Henry Sandow lent me that I asked if I might buy him. Henry agreed, and soon after I got back to Wantage I arranged for the horse to be sent to Wantage Road station by train. The whole family went to meet him, taking Harry Carvey with us. I was slightly apprehensive about Harry, remembering the story of a bishop who asked his groom to look at a horse he wanted to buy. After the inspection the bishop asked, "Well, what do you think of him?" "I don't like him, my lord," said the groom. "What don't you like about him?" "Well, I don't like his 'ocks, nor his arse, nor anything that is his." Harry Carvey, I am glad to say, was not as rude as that. He soon had Henry under control, and rode him back to Wantage.

I had several rides over the Downs on Henry, and he was certainly a pleasure to ride. But he was not as placid as Seagull, and he used to get rather too excited and wound up. To break him in gently for the hunting season I thought it would be a good idea to take him out cubbing.

And so came that fateful morning in October 1957 when we set off to a meet at Hanney. It was a cold morning, and the mist was just clearing as we rode along the Steventon road to the draw at Drayton Plantation. The ground round Hanney is particularly wet, and as we left the road we found the fields squelching with mud. Near the Plantation a farmer had recently erected a stout post-and-rail fence made of willow, and I decided to have a quick spin over the fence.

Henry was not yet used to our country after his Cornish banks, and as we approached the post-and-rails I could tell that he had misjudged his timing. He took off too far from the fence, without sufficient lift to clear it – partly, perhaps, the fault of the boggy ground. There was a dreadful crack as he hit the stout willow rail with his forefeet, and somersaulted. I was thrown head first, straight towards the ground.

I dimly recall seeing the ground come up to meet me. Then my forehead hit the ground, my neck was bent sharply backwards, Henry's huge form landed on my chest, and everything went black.

When I came to I was lying on damp grass, with no sign of Henry. I tried to get up, but my legs would not work, and then, to my horror, I found that I had no sensation anywhere below my neck. My brain was still clear, and I realised that I had severely damaged my spinal cord, either by breaking or dislocating my neck.

## Chapter 15

# Fall and a Broken Neck

A doctor will always judge the prognosis of a case by comparing it with all the similar cases he has seen. My attitude to my own case was no exception. I remembered a 20-year-old girl who had broken her neck by falling out of a farmhouse window: she had lived for four days. I remembered a publican who had broken his neck by falling down his cellar steps: he had lived for ten days.

My thoughts as I made my own diagnosis that morning remain clearly with me. My mind went back to other occasions when I had been near death – in No Man's Land below Vimy Ridge in 1915, when I had been hit by flying shrapnel, in hospital with gas gangrene and a temperature of 105 deg., in that fearful storm on the *Dinard*. On none of those occasions did I feel that I was going die – I just felt, somehow, that the world could not get on without me yet. Lying in that field with a broken neck was different. I felt quite resigned, that I had had a good run for my money, and that it was just a question of waiting for the end. Some people started gathering round me, and I heard someone suggest putting me on a sheep-hurdle and carrying me back to the road. I could still speak, and I told them on no account to try to lift me until the stretcher-bearers arrived – knowing horribly well the risk of disturbing a broken spinal column and making the damage worse. I thought of an old Colonel under whom I had served in the First World War. He fell with a bullet in his stomach, and I remembered how he had drawn his revolver and threatened to shoot any well-meaning comrade who tried to carry him back to the trenches. He knew well enough the danger of compressing the stomach after a bullet wound, and the risk of fatal peritonitis. By lying still where he was until darkness fell and the stretcher-bearers could come out, that Colonel survived.

My stretcher-bearers eventually came, and carried me carefully over the fields to the ambulance waiting in the road. I was taken to the Radcliffe Hospital in Oxford, and while I was being X-rayed, the orthopaedic consultant, an old friend, came ask how I was. "I'm finished," I said.

I had always admired patients who could accept certain death, and carry on gamely without making a fuss, and I hoped that I should be able to follow their example. The X-ray showed that I had fractured the body of my fifth cervical vertebra, and had also five broken ribs, where Henry had fallen on me. To make things easier for me, and, as it seemed, to make my last few days more comfortable, I was given fairly stiff shots of pethidine. After the pethidine my body used to get intense relief, and often I would sink into hallucinations. I can remember lying in bed and staring up at the ventilator grill in the ceiling, trying to work out what was happening to me. I had no feeling in my body, and I used to think that possibly I was already dead, and that the ventilator grill was the lid of my coffin.

Then, after about a week, I suddenly found that I could arch my back slightly as I lay in bed. I could definitely move my back, but each movement was accompanied by violent shortness of breath. It was agony to breathe, yet to get any breath at all I had to breathe as deeply as I could. My broken ribs made each breath excessively painful. I was X-rayed again, and it was found that a huge blood-clot around the vertebrae, that had been pressing on the spinal cord, had ruptured. This had poured blood into the left chest cavity, collapsing the lung and half-filling the pleural cavity with blood; but the rupture had also relieved pressure on the spinal cord. I suffered most peculiar sensations in my right leg and other parts of my body, but bits of movement gradually came back. First I could move a shoulder, then there was a flicker of movement in one hand, and at last I managed to move a finger.

Throughout all this time O. was marvellous. She used to come to the hospital early in the morning, with a book and her knitting, and either chatter gently about all the little things that were happening at home, or, if she sensed that I didn't want to talk, she would just sit cormpanionably and read. Sometimes she would write letters. She has an iron self-discipline, and will never allow any element of self-pity to creep into any situation, insisting always that regret is futile, and that every human situation should be met with positive thinking.

My own sojourn in hospital taught me many things about life as well as medicine. One lesson was how incredibly complex is the simplest of bodily actions that normally are taken for granted. Consider yawning, for instance – ordinarily one yawns without a second thought, but in reality a yawn is a most complicated affair, requiring delicate co-ordination of many different muscles. And where are your feet? Normally, you can shut your eyes and touch whichever foot you want, but if the delicate fibres taking messages to and from the brain are damaged, you lose all sense of position. I used to smile at the hospital story of a man waiting in the out-patients department to see a neurologist: he wanted to tie up his shoelace, and found that he had tied the lace of the man next to him in the queue. This is precisely what can happen – I found that I had to watch my own feet very carefully to discover just where they were.

As I acquired a scrap more movement in my body I was transferred to the Nuffield Orthopaedic Centre in another part of Oxford. Here expert physiotherapists were on hand to make sure that every flicker of movement was developed and put to use.

Just before Christmas – nearly three months after my accident – I was able to go home to Wantage. I was still having twice-nightly injections of pethidine, prescribed originally to ease my passing from the world, and I had become horribly dependent on them. It was not so much now that they relieved pain, but my whole body looked forward to them, and to the wonderful sense of relaxation that they gave. With a great effort, I first stopped the second nightly injection, and then, after about ten days, I abandoned pethidine altogether. This required a really huge effort of will, and those first few nights without pethidine made me understand the agonies that a drug addict must go through when he is being weaned of his drug. In my case, I am thankful to say, willpower worked, and I was able to give up the drug completely.

After this spell at home I went back to the Nuffield Orthopaedic Centre for more remedial exercises to assist the nerve-fibres which had been left undamaged to come back to life. By this time I could stand up with the assistance of two nurses, one on either side, and after further exercises in the gym my knees began to stop sagging and folding up like weak hinges. I had a wonderful physiotherapist, who gave me constant encouragement, and so at last enabled me to take a few steps on my own.

I came home again in February, but continued to go to the Orthopaedic Centre's gym every afternoon, to keep up my exercises. I improved steadily, but my greatest trouble was that I could not regain full feeling in my right hand – the hand which a doctor uses for everything from writing prescriptions to delicate manipulation of a patient's abdomen to discover if there is a lump of any sort in some particular area of tenderness. Years of experience had given me a kind of extra-sensitivity in my right hand, and I found the lack of this a heavy burden.

But I began to be able to walk again, and even to try driving a car. O. used to take me to a disused airfield near Wantage, where I would try driving along the empty runways. It was a good thing that they were fine, broad runways, for as my reflexes returned, the car would swerve suddenly from one verge to the other. Every day I forced myself to walk a little farther. One great day I made such a long walk that I asked O. to measure it on the mileometer of the car, feeling sure that it would come out at several miles. She put the trip indicator to zero and drove slowly over the distance I had covered; it came out as just one-quarter of a mile.

As my walking and general control improved I decided that I must think about getting back to work. Just months after my fall I took my first surgery. To start with I had some anxious moments, for procedures which would have been simple enough before had become major tasks. But my partners were wonderfully patient in helping me, and encouraging me to go on.

To celebrate my return to work we held a Resurrection Party at 2 Priory Road, inviting everybody who had helped us. I remember offering a champagne to old Harry Carvey – I can see him now, sitting at the far end of our sitting room, with his best cloth cap on his head, one hand on his left knee, the other on his upright walking stick. He declined the champagne. "Wouldn't touch the stuff – like poison to me," he said, and settled for a Mackeson.

It was a lovely evening. Harry Carvey, spurred on by "Just fancy that," from Miss Taylor, the North Country dispenser we had at the surgery, told story after story of great runs in his days with the Whaddon Chase. One grim one was of Bannister Cook, to whom Harry had been groom. Bannister had set off riding a big bay horse, but the horse had come home without him. A search revealed his master lying dead in the woods. I felt humbly how much more fortunate I had been.

Another of our guests was Mrs. Barlow, the widow of a local undertaker, who had lived all her life in a cottage next door to 2 Priory Road. She was a tremendously kind and generous person. When we had horses there was always a piece of bread on her windowsill for them, and whenever she came to the house she brought a brown paper parcel containing some titbit for our dogs. She was always coming round to help with the washing up or some other household task, and once when we offered to pay her she said "I don't want any paying – If I didn't come over to you I'd just be sitting at home looking at myself in the mirror."

We heard the locally famous story of Mrs. Barlow's visit to London. In her kindly way she had promised a neighbour to buy a roll of linoleum for her, and when she got to London it was the first thing that she did. But she hadn't realised the linoleum would be heavy. She could scarcely lift it, but she managed to get it up on her shoulder, and staggered through the streets with it like a soldier carrying his rifle at the slope. She had arranged to go to Selfridges to have lunch with her niece, who worked there as a lift attendant, but walking with the linoleum was so slow that when she finally reached Selfridges the lunch hour was over, and her niece was back on duty in her lift. Nothing daunted, Mrs. Barlow stayed in the lift, exchanging family news with her niece as they went up and down, their conversation interrupted every time they stopped and her niece had to call out "Children's Dresses', "Ladies Coats" and the rest. It was a memorable party. It gave me a chance of trying to say "Thank You", and it did me a lot of good.

As my confidence returned I was able to help a bit more in the practice, though I could still work only very slowly. I have always hated having to rely on anyone else in doing my job, but now I had no option, and I found it horribly frustrating. I had one call during those first weeks which nearly ended in disaster. This was to an elderly man who was suffering from a painful carbuncle. I struggled up the stairs to his room and decided that he ought to have an injection of penicillin. I duly gave him the injection – and then suddenly, he collapsed, falling on the floor, and dislodging his false teeth as he fell. The teeth stuck in the back of his throat, obstructing his breathing, and he began to go blue in the face. With difficulty, I knelt down on the floor beside him, and put a finger down his throat to try to hook up the teeth. At that critical moment, his wife, who was practically stone deaf, came into the room. She saw her husband unconscious on the floor, with me apparently lying on top of him with my hands on his throat. Jumping to the conclusion that I had taken leave of my senses and was trying to murder her husband, she rushed at me to pull me off. I tried desperately to explain what the trouble was, but she couldn't hear a word. Using all the strength remaining in my left arm I managed to push her away. She reeled across the room, and sat on the floor. Then, with a superhuman effort, I contrived to lift her husband on to a chair, with his head hanging down. He gave a violent cough, shot out his false teeth and to my intense relief started breathing again.

For years my sister Alice, in Australia, had been asking me to go out for a visit. In 1962, my son Dick, having qualified at St Thomas's, was able to act as a locum for me, so O and I went to Australia. We travelled on the P&O liner *Oriana*, a truly magnificent ship, and enjoyed the voyage greatly. What changes I found in Australia! Where once I had travelled laboriously by horse or camel, there were now fine motor roads, and life generally seemed to have become much more complex and sophisticated, but Australian kindliness and hospitality were unchanged, and we had a splendid holiday.

I returned to work in Wantage, helped greatly by Dick, until the autumn of 1963, when he went to India for a spell in a mission hospital there. On his return from India we appointed him an assistant in the practice – just what I had been forty years before. In 1966 I retired, and Dick became a junior partner. I had felt bitter at the start of the National Health Service over not receiving full compensation for the money I had spent to enter the practice. It was some consolation now to feel that Dick could join without having to pay anything.

Although I retired from the Health Service, I continued to see a few of my old patients privately. One was a splendid old lady at Harwell, now over 90, whom I had attended since 1923. I remember her brother cycling over one evening to ask if I would accept him and his sister as patients, and how much I would charge to visit them. I said, "It's six miles there and six miles back, so it will have to be a guinea a visit." He replied, "Excuse me, but I don't think that's quite right." He went out to look at the mileage on his cyclometer, and returned to say that the distance was only 5½ miles, so I agreed to visit them for half a guinea. Times have changed, but I still charge only one guinea, which is a good deal less than the taxi fare.

# Chapter 16

# Summing Up

What a change there has been from the general practice I entered in 1923 to the general practice I left in 1966. The advent of modern drugs revolutionised the treatment of many diseases which in the 1920s would have been long serious illnesses, possibly fatal. Antibiotics for infections, streptomycin for tuberculosis, vitamin B12 for pernicious anaemia, insulin for diabetes, and many, many others have wrought a transformation in the doctor's job. We still have a cupboard at the surgery with a row of brown earthenware jars, full of strong-smelling unguents – tar paste and other strange ingredients which were used for varying cases of dermatitis according to the whim of the GP, with little success. Now one tube of a cortisone cream can cure many such lesions in a few days.

I remember Dr Birt telling me when I first came to the surgery, "The principle of general practice, old chap, is to keep your patient amused while nature effects a cure." Often nature did not effect a cure, and we would spent long, distressing hours with our patients, administering medicines which only made their end more comfortable. I remember the medicines available in my home in Cambridge. These were phenacetin (which came in enormous cachets); malt and cod liver oil to make me fat; Parish's food to improve my sister's blood; liquorice powder to help my brother's bowels (he was the only one brave enough to swallow it); and if any of us were ill we would be given a febrifuge by Dr Deighton – heaven knows what it contained.

It may seem odd to say it, but I think that modern drugs may have contributed to the decline of the doctor-patient relationship. As we had mostly such ineffective treatments, our patients would often take a long time to improve, during which we would have to act far more as a friend and comforter than we do nowadays. Over this long period of time a strong relationship was built up. One shared in all one's patient's worries and anxieties, practically becoming one of the family. The professor who died of pernicious anaemia after fifteen years of illness would now come to the surgery at the onset of his symptoms. I would suspect pernicious anaemia, but I would take a blood sample to send to the pathology laboratory at the Radcliffe to clinch the diagnosis. He would then be given an injection of vitamin B12 each month by the district nurse, curing the condition completely. I would have had only the occasional consultation to build up my relationship, instead of 15 years.

The sheer quantity of drugs available today is colossal. We have a dozen or so drugs which work miracles, but these are produced by the drug companies under various trade names in differing combinations, so that today's index of drugs looks more like a telephone directory. The drug companies are in a unique position in that the consumer, who is the patient via his doctor, consumes their product without having to worry about cost. Sometimes, unlike the general trend with other consumer goods, where there is great rivalry to undercut prices, a drug may be more popular if it is more expensive – the idea being that if one gives a patient a more expensive preparation it will cure him more quickly. The pharmaceutical industry is a huge and affluent one – a course of antibiotics can cost £80 and a course of injections of hormones to enable a patient to achieve a pregnancy can cost £500.

We employ a secretary at the surgery to clear away the pile

of brochures and samples from the drug firms which arrive each morning, seducing us with calendars, paperweights and other gimmicky presents with the name of their product displayed on them. Nearly every day representatives from the drug companies call at the surgery, with gaily coloured graphs showing how their product is more effective than all others, and extracts from the medical journals praising their pills. The other partners would never see these representatives, as they felt that it was an immoral waste of money, forcing up the price of the drugs; but I thought of it from a slightly lower level, and knew what I would feel like if I were a representative driving away from the Wantage surgery where all the doctors had been too snooty to see me. It was certainly not much effort to sit down to listen to them for a few minutes.

An amusing invitation arrived from a drug firm the other day to a meeting in a local hotel where they offered to tell us about their latest product to help bronchitis. They promised a film entitled *Sputum* to be followed by a buffet lunch. I hope the hotel still made a profit after everyone's appetite had been well damped-down by the film.

The widespread use of the motor car has made a vast difference to the life of the GP today (and his patients). But this is not so much because of the doctor's use of the car, as because so many of his patients now have cars. When I first came to Wantage I used to do perhaps ten to twenty visits each day and see about six patients in the surgery. By the time I retired I was making about six visits to patients at home, and seeing perhaps twenty five at the morning surgery, and the same number at the evening surgery. Visiting the patient in his home is a necessary and worthwhile part of the general practitioner's job, and often it is only when one sees one's patient at home, with his family and all his personal things, that one can understand what he is really like, and how he reacts to his illness. This, for me, has always been the most important ingredient of general practice to know the patient as an individual, and not just as a number in a waiting room queue. I have always reckoned that if, during a surgery, I saw twenty patients, I could write at least two sides of foolscap about each of them. Some might think that much of what I wrote were silly details, but they were details which gave one a better understanding of one's patient. I think that the general practitioner who does not enjoy this part of his work, and who does not think it important, will be a poor sort of GP, and his life will be very boring. This personal relationship is a unique privilege, and one of the most important things that the modern GP must keep; without it, his role will be reduced, by his own fault, to that of a civil servant sorting out patients to feed the hospitals.

The reorganisation of the large hospitals has made a huge change in the life and work of a GP. The large hospitals cope now with cases which, in the past, the GP would have had to struggle with to the best of his ability, taking up many hours of his time. Twenty years ago, if I diagnosed a case of appendicitis in the home, I would take the patient to Wantage Hospital myself, take out his appendix myself, and then look after him for the next ten days myself, until he was fit to go home. It was very rewarding, but also very time-consuming. Now, my son writes a letter in the patient's house for him to take to hospital with him, stating his findings, and what diagnosis he has made, and as soon as he can he telephones the Radcliffe to let them know he has a patient with acute appendicitis, and asks the resident surgeon to admit him. He telephones the ambulance service, asking for the patient to be picked up. It is highly efficient, and the whole problem can be out of a doctor's hands in five minutes; but much less rewarding work than a doctor's job used to be.

After the reorganisation of the hospitals I carried on with some surgery, but felt increasingly that if everything went well it was for my own personal satisfaction, but that if anything went wrong, the patient might think – or even say – "You should have sent me to the big hospital, Doctor, and have it done properly by the specialist" – not realising that the "specialist" in the white coat might be the young houseman who had been qualified only a few weeks.

Wantage is privileged by the retention of its "cottage" hospital. There were some worrying moments after the introduction of the NHS when the future of such cottage hospitals was threatened, but now they can be seen to be performing a very vital role in taking some of the load off the main hospital, providing beds for patients convalescing after an operation, but mainly for the elderly and infirm.

Young people nowadays do not seem to have the same sense of responsibility that people once had for ageing parents. Children do not seem to accept that they owe their parents any debt, not only for the effort expended on them as babies, but for all the worries and anxieties they shared as they grew older. In turn, as parents grow old they need their children to care for them.

Another aspect of diminishing responsibility is the readiness with which people walk out of marriage as soon as difficulties arise, deserting their children in an utterly selfish way. People blame the "permissive society", but I think we were all pretty permissive when we were young although we did not talk about it so much. I remember during my two wars how we would dream of a Utopia when the fighting would be finished and everyone would live in peace. There would be marvellous opportunities for all classes in education, free medical treatment for all, and even if there was unemployment everyone would be given enough money on which to live. Now we have this longed-for Utopia, the welfare state, and people still are not happy. Human beings really sparkle when faced with adversity, and seem to need a goal to strive for in peace as the nation had in war.

I am a little tired now. I spend most of my afternoons sitting in my car on the edge of the Downs, with a magnificent view across the Vale of the White Horse towards Oxford. I should like to get out of the car and go for a long walk along the Ridgeway, but my body is tired, and my legs don't work as well as they did before my accident.

My favourite place to park the car is a small cinder track running through Segsbury Camp, and then steeply down the hill, sunken through generations of use, towards Letcombe Regis, where the Downland water gushes out of the chalk feeding the ancient watercress beds, to meander on through Wantage until it finally joins the Thames. In this ancient place I reflect on all the people who have passed this way, from the iron age people to Jude the Obscure in Hardy's novel who came down this same cinder track over 100 years ago from Mary Green (Fawley) on his way to see his aunt in Cresscombe (Letcombe). As he came over the brow of the hill, and saw this magnificent view before him, with the hill above Oxford in the distance, he was full of hopes and excitement for his future, but fate was not very kind to him.

Fate has been kinder to me, so I can look over the Vale with rather different thoughts. To the left I can see Faringdon Folly, built on a rounded hill above Faringdon. At the foot of the hill there used to be the Old Berks Hunt Point-to-Point course, and I remember the first and last time I ever rode in a point-to-point. Beyond Faringdon Folly, I can see the Cotswolds, and on a clear day I can even see the hill beyond Burford, about 30 miles away. I remember the fun I had with Jan Morphew hunting in the Heythrop country. I cannot see Oxford but I know it is there, and I think sometimes of the inspiration of the men who built Oxford 900 years ago, hauling the best quality Cotswold stone from the Taynton quarries at Burford for the corners, and then filling in with the poorer quality local stone.

What an enormous change the canals in their day must have

made to people's lives. Oxford buildings could now be built and patched by stone from farther afield, gently floated up a canal, instead of the toil of hauling weighty blocks with horse and waggon along deep cart tracks. If only people today would respect, or understand, the sheer human effort involved in building some of the ancient buildings which are so readily pulled down by property developers on the pretext of progress. With one flick of a bulldozer modern demolition gangs will smash down craftsmanship which cannot be repeated or replaced. How hurt the craftsmen of a hundred years ago would feel if they could see the destruction of their work. I remember an old lady who lived in a thatched cottage and whom I often used to visit. I said to her once. "How lovely and peaceful your cottage is." "I am so glad you like it," she replied. "My family keeps telling me I should move into one of the modern Council bungalows, but I sit in my front room and look at the beam going through, and think it's not quite straight, but very nearly straight, it was sawn out by hand, and the man who sawed it out of a tree 400 years ago tried very hard to get it straight for me. If I was in a Council bungalow the beam would be straight, but it would have been sawn by a machine which would not have thought about me at all."

The canals have gone now. Below me lies the sadly overgrown course of the Wilts and Berks Canal, which brought Somerset coal to the district and took away agricultural produce. What an excitement this must have been to the men who planned it – the thought of a boat travelling overland from London to Bath! How sad it is that people should treat its path now as a nuisance, or as a long open trench, where they can throw old bedsteads, old prams, and rusty old pieces of motor car. This canal should surely be respected as something very special, not only because of its history, but because of its modern value as a huge, long lake, lined by willow trees, the home of moorhens and wild ducks. It should be an area where people can walk, or sit down and pause to think a bit about what they are doing, and how they are living.

There is a band of enthusiasts who have worked with amazing determination and foresight in clearing the Kennet and Avon canal. They understand its value. When my daughter Judy came over from South Africa, we hired a horse-drawn barge on the Kennet and Avon near Newbury to celebrate her engagement and were hauled gently through the cut cornfields and through the locks and back in the moonlight, the only sound being the clump of the shire horse's hooves on the towpath, the noise of the reeds disturbed by the wake of the boat, and the occasional moorhen and water rat. This is one sort of enterprise that the Government should be supporting.

The Great Western Railway also lies below me, following a similar course to the canal. I enjoy thinking about this in the same way – the excitement of those who built it, and how it must have affected the life of the region.

I can't see the Thames, but I can see the Wittenham Clumps, away over to the right, which marks the course of the Thames by Wallingford as it winds its way to the Goring Gap – that gap where the water which used to cover the countryside below me suddenly eroded its way through the soft chalk, bursting out and forming the Thames as it drained to the North Sea.

Thinking about the Thames I look back on the happy times I have had with my brother Stenie, gently punting up and down its waters on a hot summer's day, with the dragonflies hovering, the damp smell of the river, the rushes, the trees with their branches trailing in the water, and the cows on the banks with their hooves squelching in mud. Afterwards we would retire to the Barley Mow for a quiet pint of beer, where Jerome K. Jerome before me used to like to stay, enjoying the peace of the Thames and getting inspiration for his novels.

My eyes leave the Wittenham Clumps and travel closer, and I see the afternoon light falling on the new cooling towers of the power station at Didcot (Didcot Cathedral?) and on the atomic energy buildings at Harwell. Are these monuments symbolising the future of the area?

How much one learns! And how exhausting it is to think of starting again. What advice can I give? I think one of the most important things in life is to grab with both hands any opportunity of doing something different. Some very small thing can change the course of one's whole life. If, in 1923, when Harold Allen asked me to join his party for the Grand National I had done the sensible thing, and said I ought to finish revising for my finals the following week, I should not have met George Witherby. If, when George Witherby had asked if I would like to join him at the Bear in Wantage for a week's hunting, I had not accepted, I might never have come to Wantage. I can think of hundreds of other occasions when some little bit of extra effort, instead of sitting at home and waiting for excitement to land on my lap, has paid off.

I think of the enormous changes and variety in my life and count myself lucky to have survived two world wars in spite of many hairy moments.

I have witnessed the simplicity of pre-war rural life, met many wonderful people from all walks of life and lived to see the incredible achievement of landing men on the moon which one could never believe possible in those far off days.

I have been truly fortunate to have had such an interesting (sometimes too interesting) life.